Nothing For Granted

. . . stepping stones to God

Peter Timmins

ISBN 0-9695601-2-5

Printed and bound in Canada
1 2 3 4 5 6 7 8 MM

Distributed by Michael Peter Timmins

Credits: Quotes from Catholishm, © by Richard P. McBrien
              and published by Haper Collins Publishers
              reproduced with their permission

The manuscript for this book was prepared and submitted to the author in
electronic form. Text composition in Garamond and display type in Kaufman
using Adobe Pagemaker® ver. 6.5 for windows®

Document preperation for electronic form by Patricia Lafreniere & Nancy Gallie
Cover and Interior Text prepared by H.M. Fichten

In Memory

R.E. "Dick" Paré
1920-1991
"He kept the love of God alive in his heart
and entered into paradise"

Table of Content

Acknowledgements

Preface

Acknowledgements

In the process of writing this book I have drawn extensively upon homilies preached over the past forty years. In the preparation of these homilies, I made use of numerous published sources. I remain grateful to their authors and hope that while frequently adapting their ideas and benefiting from their scholarship, I have not plagiarized their material. Wherever I have knowingly employed a direct quotation, I have identified the passage as such.

My sincere thanks to all who have encouraged me in this project, and especially to Patricia Lafrenière and Nancy Gallie for their valuable help toward its final realization.

PREFACE

My primary intention in writing this book is not to prove, nor even to instruct, but, quite simply, to share a series of reflections upon that which I both feel and know to be at the centre of my being and of yours.

I am neither a scholar nor a mystic. I am a parish priest. After almost forty years of preaching sermons and homilies, I have come to realize that I have taken too much for granted. That is to say, I have generally presumed a whole parcel of basic common denominators, which together formed a shared platform upon which I could build with my listeners. To be more specific, I presumed that once enunciated, the word GOD would trigger the same images and concepts in just about everyone's mind and that the same could be said for words like SPIRIT, REDEEMER and GRACE.

Frankly, I don't chastise myself for being overly presumptuous because the very nature of my ministry leaves no choice. For example, what good does it do me to know that the word GOD probably conjures up almost as many images as there are people present?

Clearly a preacher has to start somewhere. Without regularly assuming some common ground, he could never get off first base. This becomes all the more apparent when you consider that the preacher in question is already limited by the contextual elements of the liturgy, not to mention the clock.

The following chapters are, then, at least to some extent, the fruit of my own frustration, for in them, I have attempted to do something which I have not succeeded in doing from the pulpit . . . to share the GOOD NEWS while, at the same time, taking nothing for granted. In order to accomplish this, I begin with the most basic observations of my environment and gradually, step by step, share a philosophical notion of a Creator-God which I believe to be authentic. I then pursue the content of what I perceive as God's revelation of self in the Old Testament. I include John the Baptist and give emphasis to Messianic expectations, as well as to the general religious, political and social scene of the day.

There follows what I believe to be the heart of this book . . . a Gospel- inspired, disciple's eye-view of Jesus' daily life. The reader is invited to start from the beginning and assume nothing about the nature and role of Jesus, but rather do what he or she has been asked to do from the outset . . . take nothing for granted. Eventually we turn to the Acts of The Apostles and to a consideration of Jesus as Messiah and then as DIVINE Messiah.

The hopefully shared affirmation of Jesus as the Divine Messiah leads to a selective reconsideration of His life, which, in the light of His divinity, can teach us so much, so very much, about God. Within this context are treated simply and briefly such important questions as evil, original sin, the role of law, redemption and God's enduring presence in this world. The work concludes with some personal reflections on eternal life, faith, providence, trust and worship.

Throughout this book, I have tried to share my beliefs and to do so in the simplest possible terms, without attempting to go into depth in any one subject. I am not a scholar and this book is certainly not intended for scholars. It is for the average man and woman and its appeal is to the emotions as well as to the intellect. Like a painter of landscapes, I frequently return to the same area of the "canvas" in order to add a new dimension or detail, in the hope that, little by little and step by step, an image of God and His relationship to us emerges from the pages in a manner which calls forth a positive response from open hearts and minds.

PREFACE TO THE SECOND EDITION

This book was originally published by the author in 1991. Three thousand copies were sold and otherwise distributed.

I have decided to publish a second edition for two reasons, the first being that I have been encouraged by both reader reaction and continuing interest. The second is that I am happy to have the opportunity to alter the format and fine-tune the text.

Peter   Timmins
Montreal

April, 2000

By the same author

The Candle
and
the Flame

The Candle
and
the Flame

A parish priest reflects upon his
church and ministry . . .

Father Peter Timmins

Chapter I

Fields and forests are beginning to show the early signs of fall. The dramatic colours, tied together by subtle tones, will soon inspire countless artists, photographers, and yes, me. I love this land, with its vast openness and its secret shady retreats, its warm sounds and its damp smells. I value the oneness with nature, the deeply-rooted awareness of which was exemplified in the native peoples, who knew this same land so many years ago. Overhead, a slightly fluctuating V-formation of Canada geese, its members chattering like excited school children, arrows its way southward. The vibrations are both strong and good. I know that I am somehow truly part of all of this. I marvel at it: every blade of grass, every feather, contains countless secrets, mysteries of nature yet unsolved. Instinctively, I know I am somehow more than a leaf, more than a bird, for I have named them and that is significant. And when it comes to being a vessel of mystery, I know that I and my kind are unsurpassed.

I know that beyond the blade of grass there is a level of higher existence. I know this because I see the birds and I hear them. I know, too, that beyond them is yet another level, for to this extent I know myself and of what I am capable. But beyond me? Beyond me, I have seen nothing, tasted nothing, smelled nothing, touched nothing, heard nothing. What does this mean?

It would appear to mean that we are, at least up to the present time, the ultimate beings. If this is so, then it would follow that everything which we see, taste, hear, smell and feel must be definable in terms of ourselves, at least so it seems to me.

I see the earth and its inhabitants as being structured according to qualitative levels, and every step up reflects a being superior in its complexity to the one on the step below. This is clearly true for the broadest categories, those of mineral, vegetable, brute animal and rational animal. From what I understand, it is also true in all of the subdivisions of the major categories, with the only exception being the category of rational animal, or man. There are no subcategories in mankind. One is either a rational animal and thus, a human being, or one is not.

Man stands apart. He is unique; yet, at the same time, contained within him is all the potential of all the other categories which we have mentioned. But, you might well object, man cannot fly like a bird, burrow like a mole, live in the watery depths like a fish. True, but nor does he have to. Dramatic as these feats are, they are not essential to man, who because of his intellect and his ability to mine and refine, design and construct, can fly in aeroplanes, operate subways, and cruise about in ships and boats on and beneath the seas.

The fact of the matter is, we truly dominate this planet. Because of our physical characteristics, we are related to every living and nonliving thing, but all of them combined together do not begin to approach the human state. For this reason, everything on earth, from a drop of water to the ape at the zoo, fits into a qualitative hierarchical order and its relative position in that order is dependent upon its resemblance to you and me. We are observably at the top of the heap, unchallenged. Individually, we are sometimes tormented, wounded and even killed by beings of the lower orders, from microbes to lions, but we are never mastered, never supplanted. For better or worse we are in charge, in command. We are that against which everything else is measured.

Then why, why do I feel so weak in the face of a North Atlantic gale? Why so small beneath the starlit sky? Why so helpless before an open grave? Why, in spite of all, do I get the distinct feeling that although I am in charge, it is of someone else's planet? I think that it is because, although I am comfortable with being part of the elite of the planet Earth, I know that I am not its cause nor, for that matter, the cause of anything on it. I am disposer, fabricator, builder, designer, trainer, composer, but I am not creator. In other words, I bring nothing into existence. As far as the eye can see, I am the elite of existence, but I am not the cause of existence. I stand tallest in someone else's garden; indeed I am the gardener, but reason tells me that the garden is not mine, and that my authority is thus limited and delegated by another. Who or what is this other? The words "force" and "power" come to mind.

The signs, as I read them, point to a superior, invisible, inaudible and, in effect, imperceptible creative force which at once constitutes and limits me.

Is this force intelligent and wilful, or is it mindless and without purpose?

Does it continue to exert itself, or was it expended in one creative blast?

What is its origin? As the grass and animals have something in common with me, do I have anything in common with "the Force?"

We are not the first to ask these questions, and we will not be the last. What is important is that each one of us must reach toward his or her own conclusion, or admit to not caring about whom and what we are. What I am trying to do in these first pages is to pose and answer these questions for myself, within a framework which for now is devoid of faith or tradition. I am not trying to prove anything to myself or to you. I am simply looking to have and share a more profound experience and awareness of that which we tend to take for granted as having been settled once and for all in Grade Two. And so, back to our fundamental quest.

If you are with me thus far, you will agree that some force, some superior, imperceptible, creative force, must be included in any authentic explanation of reality. No thinking person can seriously believe in a man-made universe. Many good and intelligent people do believe that there is no intelligent force beyond our own human species. They are of the opinion that material forces, which we do not fully understand, formed and continue to form our universe, that it is from these formations that all of nature, including ourselves, has evolved.

Like most of you, I have neither the expertise nor the will to sift through all of the theories of the origin of the universe, and of the life it contains and supports. I do not, however, dismiss them out of hand, for they are often the work of brilliant minds and honest questioning, and they contain valid insights. However, there are, quite simply, some things that I know instinctively. For example, when I listen to a great violin concerto, I know in the very depths of my being that I am not the result of a series of explosions, accidental molecular combinations and selective breeding. There is something within me which responds passionately to beauty, goodness, and yes, truth, something which cries out in celebration of my dignity. I know that I am not an accident. It may seem to you that I am beginning to lose my objectivity, but for the time being, suffice it to say that history bears ample witness to the fact that commonly experienced insights such as mine are not to be taken lightly.

If, then, as I firmly believe, I am not an accident, it follows that I am intended by a consequently intelligent, creative force.

Thus, observation and experience, coupled with reason and instinct, have brought us, I hope, together, to the recognition of a super-intelligent, imperceptible, creative force. This is a truly awesome concept: awesome, but frustrating. It is frustrating because it would be so much easier if we could see the force, taste it, smell it, feel it and hear it. Nevertheless, we know that it must exist, because its effects cry out so loudly for a cause unlike any other. If it were a material force, it would follow that at least one or more of our senses would be able to lock onto it. But the fact is that only our minds, only our intellects, can be applied to this particular reality. So the force must be immaterial, or, in other words, spiritual. The material world points to its existence, and yet its existence remains independent of matter and the rules governing it. This mysterious force, by virtue of being immaterial, cannot decay, die or cease to be. Where did it come from? When did it come into existence?

As I see it, to presume that it came from anywhere, or that it had a beginning, simply contradicts its identity as THE creative force. If indeed it did have a source and a cause, then we should logically judge it to be of only passing interest and concentrate on efforts to identify ITS source and cause, and so on and so on, until we arrive at where we are right now.

The fact remains that it is difficult for us to imagine our creative force as having no beginning and no end, as being eternal. In truth, this is not merely difficult, it is impossible. So where do we go from here?

We make every effort to put our imaginations on hold. Imagination is wonderfully entertaining and productive, but it has no place in this particular phase of our quest. It is, in fact, a major hindrance. Imagination refers to images and pictures which are very helpful for designing clothes, identifying a gadget or writing a novel, but totally misleading when applied to that which, by its very nature, cannot be imaged or pictured, cannot be imagined. Is it then possible to learn of the unimaginable? Yes, it is. By turning down our imaginations and turning up our intellects.

It is my belief that an eternal creative force, although unimaginable, is by no means inconceivable. In other words, I can conceive of such a force even though I cannot imagine it. To do so, however, I must shift up to my highest human gear, and with my eyes and mouth closed, with my hands joined, surrounded by silence, apply my reason, without images, to the questions at hand. This is not easy! We are designed to do this, but most of us are mentally lazy. The route we are following and the goal we have set demand that we make this effort to be, for want of a better expression, fully human, truly rational.

Our horizons are broad indeed, because, generally speaking, anything is conceivable so long as it does not contain a contradiction. Thus, for example, a square circle is inconceivable, but what about an eternal, intelligent, creative force? Is it conceivable? Why not? There is no contradiction.

Personally, I have become convinced that no other explanation of our universe makes sense, and that any theory appearing to contradict this avoids the fundamental question, because it presumes the existence of certain primitive energies, cells, forces and locations, then proceeds to develop a non-creational theory.

You and I, on our pilgrimage toward truth, cannot afford to take anything for granted, and so we are impelled to apply our minds to the eternal primary force, which caused to become, or created, the first seeds of all of that which is.

Chapter II

The innate certainty of my being the result of intention and not accidents, as well as the intricate patterns of cause and effect that are observable in nature, whether within the context of evolution or not, argue, as we suggested earlier, for a super intelligence: not a blind force, but a purposeful, rational being. And so the time seems to have come for us to drop the word "Force."

But wait! Unless I miss my guess, there goes the old imagination, triggered by the word BEING, already conjuring up human-like images of a localized entity. That is why I clung for so long to "Force." We must try hard not to imagine this BEING, but only to consider its nature. Clearly it is the ultimate BEING, the absolute reality, the ultimate intelligent BEING, the eternal creator.

So many questions that habitually come to mind make no sense in the light of what we have already considered. Questions such as, What does it look like? Is it male or female? But other questions are in order, such as, Does it continue to exert itself? or Was its creative power expended in one creative act? Why did the CREATOR create in the first place? Is this being a person? Does it have a name? And there are the very big questions, As an intelligent creature of an intelligent creator, where do I fit in? How do I relate to and reflect my creator? What, if anything, is expected of me? How does His plan and my potential relate to each other?

Creation differs from art insofar as creation is the bottom line. There are no tools, no materials. It is not the modification of what already is, but rather the bringing into being from nothingness. And this leads up to an important question, Once the creature is brought into being, what keeps it from ceasing to be, or in other words, what maintains it in a state of being?

A table remains a table, as long as it keeps its form and for as long as the material from which it is made is not in some way destroyed. So, the continuing existence of the table is dependent upon the shape and condition of the underlying material, or that from which it was made. But what would keep it in existence if it were made from nothing, if it were created? Clearly, only the will of its creator, who brought it into being in the first place, is capable of maintaining it in existence. If I stood before you in an empty room and willed into existence a table, it would not be surprising to you if I were able to will it out of existence just as easily. And if I chose not to will it out of existence, you would rightly assume that it was being maintained in existence because that was the way I wanted it. The reason your assumption would be correct is that by definition, a creator's will is the underlying force maintaining anything which is the result of an act of creation. In reality, everything has its roots in creation, even the table of which we spoke. Everything is but a link in the chain which finally hangs on the hook of creation. You could say that being the creator and being the author of all existence is one and the same thing. Now this concept is hard for us to understand, because we are not accustomed to thinking in terms of a common source of existence linking everything which is. But this is a vital and fundamental concept, as it colours our view of the entire universe, not to mention of ourselves.

Although we are made into something, we are made out of nothing. This makes the term "self-sufficient" a joke. We are totally dependent, as is everything else that can trace its roots to creation, which means literally everything else. The more I think of it, the more I want to "pray," to establish some kind of hopefully friendly contact with this creator, upon whom my every breath ultimately depends and whose will must define my significance.

Through regeneration, existence is passed on from generation to generation. But whether we consider a man, a tree, or a table, the trail into the past will lead to one or more creative acts by a single uncreated being whose gift of existence supports the whole universe. Once again, this is hard for us to accept, because it is beyond our imaginations, beyond, if you will, our wildest dreams. Pause for a while. Does what we are saying make sense? If not, why not?

Most modern scientists agree that the universe is based upon a reasonable plan which is both intricate and subtle. Those who support the "big bang" theory understand the earth to be the product of stardust, the debris of the "big bang." They further maintain that carbon chemistry in the oceans gave rise to living organisms. Yet, according to one prominent secular source, the discoveries of Hubble and Einstein, when taken together, give empirical validation to the notion of a creation event, which, in turn, leads to the "breathtaking idea" that everything in the universe could have arisen from literally nothing.

Thus, a rightly cautious scientific community neither affirms nor denies a creator. It follows that in our affirmation of a creator, we are not going against any hard evidence of modern cosmology. What we are doing is taking that next step which is said by scientists to be the exclusive realm of theologians.

And so we find ourselves in a theological environment, and the theologian says to us, "I understand where you are coming from, and I'd like to join you as you move forward because this BEING whom you are gradually discovering is the focal point of my discipline. I call this Being by the ancient Anglo-Saxon name 'GOD'."

And so that word GOD, so encumbered by and encrusted with the barnacles of misconception and imagination, is once again before us. But now we have soaked it, cleansed it, purified it to the point where we can agree upon what it means. We can take that creator being which we have discovered together and say, "This is what I call GOD." We do this with mixed emotions, because on the one hand we are beginning to feel the pain of loss, the loss of a GOD whom we have created in our image, a GOD who sees, hears and occasionally speaks as we do. But, on the other hand, we are encouraged by the unfolding of a new understanding which promises untold enrichment. However, for the moment, all we can say is that He is the ultimate reality, the CREATOR, He who is; that He is eternal, spiritual, intelligent; that He is imperceptible to our senses, but not to our minds, and therefore, not a fit object of our imaginations, but only of our intellects. Furthermore, we can assert that as everything which "is" can ultimately be traced back to nothingness, it follows that it exists at this moment only because He so permits. This, for the moment, then, is our understanding of GOD. Upon this we agree. And I hope that, so far at least, we have taken nothing for granted. Remember, I have not proven the existence of GOD. I have simply shared with you my confidence in a perception of reality, because in the final analysis, belief or unbelief appear to be a question of confidence or non confidence.

Before moving on to a more specific discussion of our subject, I want to share a thought with you on the role of intuition in our quest for GOD. We touched on this earlier, but I would like to elaborate at this point. We have emphasized the role of reason and the need to control imagination. But perhaps the most important element of all is intuitive knowledge. We seem to have a natural tendency to reach out toward that which is beyond us and respond to it. This, in fact, probably explains why you are taking the time and trouble to read these pages. Earlier in this work, I stated that there is something within me that cries out in celebration of my dignity. I simply know that I am not an accident. I know that I am intended, like the flower that responds to the sun, like the violin that responds to the bow, that there is that within me which, as St. Paul expressed it, cries out "ABBA, FATHER."

Not very convincing? Perhaps not to some, but my point is that, when all is said and done, to me, nothing is more convincing than the doubts and misgivings that beset me, when, for whatever reason, that voice is stilled within me. Of course, I can fall back on all of the firm philosophical and theological foundations and conclusions which are the fabric of my intellectual life as a priest, and for a time this does sustain me, but it doesn't move me, encourage me, make me cry out, "FATHER." Intuitive experience of God, although it is not likely to win debates, is essential if our knowledge of God is to go beyond theory and speculation, and enter into the realm of relationship. I have often observed that prospective converts to Catholicism, who have had no religious education of any kind, have come to see me because they already believe in the fundamentals. They have, in other words, confidence in their intuitive appreciation of the contradiction between their own purposefulness on the one hand, and the notion of a GOD-less world on the other. As we move through these pages together, I beg you to trust and respect your intuitions. They are valid and in complete harmony with your rationality.

Somewhere along the line, we posed the question, "Did creation take place in one creative event, or does the CREATOR continue, to this day, to exert His creative energies?" I think that we saw the answer to that question in our consideration of God's continuing to maintain all things in existence in one form or another, and so, in a sense, making of creation an ongoing reality. But, as I understand it, nothing new is being created except the individual soul of every newly-conceived child. Each one is, as it were, touched by the hand of the CREATOR.

We humans attribute to the Creator a name, be it GOD, ALLAH, JEHOVAH, YAHWEH, etc., and we refer to God as HE, but is God a person? And why HE? No, God is not a person. Strictly speaking, God is not even a "being" because God is not an "anything." Being "something" would contain and limit Him. God is unique and, therefore, ideally to be spoken of in a unique language. But to be practical, we must use popular vocabulary if we are going to dialogue about God, and in this process we must realize and accept the inherent

11

limitations and inaccuracies of such vocabulary. Frankly, I have little patience with people who get hung up on theological accuracy to such an extent that they can use only the most uncommon language to express a reality which is common to every facet of existence. For example, while it is accurate to say that God does not have hands, it is still true to say that God has the whole world "in His hands." And while we are on the subject, why HE, HIS, HIM? Well, clearly, from our point of view, "IT" would be unacceptable . Our only other alternative would be SHE or HER. And why not? Again, the danger here is in letting our imaginations slip into gear and produce all sorts of distortions, like the image of the white-bearded figure who sits on clouds, has a very deep voice and is partial to red and white flowing robes.

What is far more authentic and, consequently, productive, is to concentrate upon the known attributes of God which we can recognize as being, at least to some extent, although only by reflection, in ourselves.

We are intelligent creatures of the intelligent Creator. Only a human being can contemplate his or her existence, purpose and death. We know that we resemble the Creator insofar as we have an intellect and a will, the proper objects of which are truth and goodness. And so, learning about ourselves helps us to understand something of the nature of God, and learning about God helps us to understand ourselves. It is precisely this element of rationality that sets us apart from the rest of the animal world.

We are capable of seeking and achieving truth and goodness. All of our other gifts, talents and attributes are in place to serve this double-faceted principal purpose.

When we get down to basics, who knows what is good and what is true? Has any one or group of us the natural right to stand above the rest and proclaim what is to be considered true and what is to be accepted as good? Clearly, we need help. We need help from the only superhuman intellectual being of which we know, the being who has created us in His image. As the saying goes, "God only knows."

Does God leave us on our own to muddle along, or has He communicated with us, told us as it were, more about Himself than we would have been able to deduct? Has He told us more about ourselves and about truth and goodness? There are many among us who believe that He has, and so, as the stated primary purpose of this work is to reflect upon the meaning of God, our focus for now will be that which God has revealed about Himself.

Chapter III

God-consciousness seems to be ingrained in human nature. Although there have always been those who claimed not to believe in God, they have usually been the exceptions. And even they put their faith and hope in something which can ultimately be identified as a God-substitute, whether it be wealth, power, prestige, beauty, health or some combination of these things.

Man, in his primitive nomadic state, was kept busy just staying alive. The search for food, shelter and clothing left little time for religious or cultural activities. "Gods" such as the sun and the moon were viewed with deference and placated, but it was only with the advent of agriculture and the domestication of animals that communities became more permanent, and thus, complex. With this complexity came the dedication of time and personnel to activities other than gathering and hunting food. Among the occupations which emerged was that of priest. By definition, a priest is one who offers sacrifice in the name of the community.

Apart from being charged with the cultic aspects of community life, priests were also consulted as to what they believed to be the gods' desires and intentions. Being human, the priests surrounded themselves with an air of mystery and power through robes and other paraphernalia, such as the bones of the dead. No doubt, as is the case today, there was among them a number of charlatans, but there were also those who were sincere in their efforts to build bridges between the finite and the infinite, between man and the personification of forces beyond his control. Were, then, all of these ancient priests either wily or ignorant? We have no right to assume that this was the case. I have no trouble in accepting the probability that the God which we have discovered could have nursed our ancestors through the instrumentality of those primitive seekers of truth. Those who believed what they were taught because they had confidence in their teachers were no less people of faith than we are today, and no less children of God. The question is, how valid was their concept of God and of Divine will? Since God is an objective reality, one can be wrong about Him, as well as right. There are no moral implications here, it is simply a question of working with what you have.

Most of you who are reading this share in my faith heritage, which is that of the Judeo-Christian tradition. I think that it is vital for us to realize that there are other valid traditions. No one tradition, including our own, can be proven to be more valid than another. It is a question of familiarity, perceived richness and confidence in the historicity and integrity of the tradition. And perhaps most significantly, it is a matter of how it responds to and deepens our own personal intuitions.

I believe the Judeo-Christian tradition to have within it the complete essence of God's revelation. But I cannot prove that to be the case any more than I could prove before that God even exists. I hasten to add that I also believe that I have much to learn from the manner in which divine truth is exposed and lived in other traditions, particularly those of the Far East, which emphasize the many manifestations of God in nature. Now, if to my fellow Catholics all of this sounds radically different from what they believe they were taught, I can only refer to Saint Ambrose, who in the 4th century wrote: "All truth, no matter by whom it is uttered, comes via the Holy Spirit."

This would seem an appropriate time to pay homage to the great Greek philosophers who, having witnessed the demise of many gods, gods whose existence depended upon primitive fears which had gradually given way to scientific understanding, began, three to five hundred years before Christ, to ask the deeper questions: questions relating to the nature of being, truth, goodness, happiness and the infinite and the finite. In this way, they gave expression to concepts upon which we earlier reflected: for example, causality, order and intention in nature. They made great strides, but they were still left with major questions. The perfect being which they and we discovered through reflection gives no answer to absurdity, to pain, to death. How, they asked, are we to imagine an infinite being who preserves in being all that is good and beautiful, and, at the same time, all that is hateful and repugnant? Even now, complete answers to these questions are not within our grasp. Partial answers are, however, within the scope of our quest, and so, in time, we will return to these and other vexing questions.

The process in which we are involved is not one in which God coyly gives us a glimpse here and there of His being and purpose, while we, not unlike teased puppies, jump and grab at whatever we can. Rather, it is a process in which our groping quest for God is animated by God's quest for man. That, you see, is the whole point of revelation. God wants us to find Him, to know Him. Revelation means to remove the veil. It is God's self-disclosure.

Revelation is commonly transmitted by means of authoritative records; for example, the Koran and the Bible. It is important to note that the "revealed" contents of these records cannot be verified. Thus, we have the basis for the tension between faith and reason, which in turn gives rise to the question, "Is it reasonable to give assent to what is apparently authoritative revelation?" I suggest that the answer is YES. To a great extent, human reason can discern the credibility of revelation. At least, we can separate the sense from the nonsense, the trustworthy from the untrustworthy, and decide for ourselves whether or not it is reasonable to place our confidence in this or that proposed source. The next step is faith. But because of the previous step, it is not an unreasonable faith: possibly erroneous, but not unreasonable, not an unreasonable placing of one's confidence.

When we speak of revelation, we are speaking of a dialogue of which God is the initiator. Strictly speaking, revelation is His message given to particular people at particular times. Our response is faith.

We perceive Divine revelation as having begun with the events described in the Old Testament of the Bible. The principal message of the Old Testament is that God has revealed Himself to all mankind in nature and in history. The history with which we are immediately concerned is that of the Hebrew people.

The people of the Bronze Age, the period stretching from 2,000 to 1,500 B.C., have been described as a nomadic hoard possessing neither ethnic nor political unity. When it comes to this era, history is almost silent, except for some glimpses into the lives of the men and women who inhabited what is now the northwest corner of Syria, close to the Turkish border. Our knowledge of these people is based upon the book of Genesis. Biblically speaking, the Bronze Age is known as the age of the patriarchs, principally of Abraham, Isaac and Jacob.

In keeping with our determination to take nothing for granted, we ought now to address the question of the credibility of the Bible. Is it historically valid? The Old Testament books of the Bible constitute a well-corroborated history of a people. The now-famous Dead Sea scrolls, which date back to the time of Jesus, enable experts to reconstruct the history of Palestine from the 4th century B.C. In recent years, great strides have been made in archaeological research, and in particular, in methods of establishing the exact dates and composition of various artifacts. One of the results is that it is now possible to demonstrate that the descriptive narratives of Genesis and Exodus concerning the migration of Abraham and his people are incredibly accurate. Study after study seems to indicate the reliability of the Old Testament as a valid account of the history of a people, the Hebrew people, and of their interpretation of that history up to the time of Jesus.

Although the sequence of historical events is not likely to give us problems, the interpretation of these events is another

17

matter. The Jews were and are a God-centred people. Their history is also the history of their understanding of their very particular relationship with God. They were the only people of antiquity who believed that they had the supreme religious duty of remembering, and therefore of recording, their past. This fact in itself is a very strong argument for the reliability of these records. Clearly, Divine interventions into Jewish history cannot be scientifically verified; however, if you remove the God-man dialogue from Old Testament history, the entire fabric collapses into illogical, unmotivated, inexplicable loose ends.

Ultimately, each one of us has to decide whether we are willing to trust the Old Testament books as a source of Divine revelation. Knowing their history, knowing how carefully the oral traditions were transmitted from generation to generation, knowing that these texts are the result of an unbroken tradition, the substance of which formed the very heart of a nation, do we creatures, when we read them, feel, sense, recognize the Creator? I do. Not always, but frequently enough to be convinced that this is no ordinary literary work. There is much in the Old Testament that I still do not really understand, and some of it I find more tiring than inspiring. But I have no trouble putting that down to ignorance and lack of insight on my part. After all, generations of scholars representing many traditions continue to draw new inspiration from these strangely inexhaustible sacred texts.

I am sure that the Muslim believer feels the same way when he reads the Koran, and I have no doubt that God has revealed Himself within those sacred texts, as well as within a number of others. Remember Saint Ambrose? "All truth no matter by whom it is uttered, comes via the Holy Spirit."

And so, back to Abraham, one of my favourite people, and I guess one of God's, too. Somewhere around 1,600 B.C., a Bedouin sheik named Abraham, gathered his tribe around the campfire and spoke of moving on to better pasture lands. The goats and the other animals upon which the tribe depended for survival were beginning to grow thin. The scene was not an unusual one. These were nomadic people, who were almost constantly on the move, although they always stayed within the same general territory. To go beyond the long-defined boundaries would be to invite trouble from similar, but hostile, tribes. Life was already difficult enough. Childbirth, disease, wild animals, drought, famine, desert storms, all took their toll with almost systematic regularity. To risk battle in another tribe's territory was to risk annihilation.

Dependent upon nature's whims, Abraham and his family and friends were inclined toward superstition, and the worshipping of a multitude of gods. For everything that was vital or beyond their personal control, there was a god: a god of rain, a god of fire, a god of fertility, and so on. Sacrifices of appeasement were frequent and brought some degree of consolation, but never the lush pasture lands and the wealth of many healthy children, which constituted the communal dream of every Semite tribe. Such were the circumstances when Abraham, standing before his tent, with the camp silent and asleep, after having prepared for the morning's departure, heard the voice of God. The Judeo-Christian age of revelation had begun.

Chapter IV

We do not know precisely how God communicated with Abraham. Somehow He made Himself known to him. It could have been via the senses or through extrasensory means. Whatever the case, Abraham was convinced that he had been reached by a supernatural being whose objective reality was very convincing.

God asked a great deal from Abraham. He asked him to accept Him as the one true God. This was not easy for a man who had a genuine fear of many gods. He asked Abraham to leave familiar pasture lands for unknown hostile territories. His promises were, however, very tempting: lush pastures and numerous descendants. Abraham was faced with a difficult decision. Should he risk his peoples' future, and indeed, their lives, on the basis of this apparent revelation which he alone had experienced? His burden of responsibility must have been extreme. We are told quite simply that Abraham put his faith in the Lord. In their turn, his family and tribe put their faith in him and in the revelation which he alone had received, but which had been given to him for them.

The next day, they moved out in search of the Promised Land, the Chosen People tentatively holding the hand of a god they had only just met. A people of faith, they believed because they had confidence in Abraham, just as children believe because they have confidence in parents and in teachers. Abraham believed because . . . well, perhaps that remains his own secret. It would seem that God had asked him to be His friend and he had said yes.

Most of us find it hard to relate to this kind of dialogue, especially if it lacks an aural or visual component, as could well have been the case with God and Abraham. But today, as never before, we are being presented with evidence of people communicating at a purely spiritual level. There have been countless documented examples of ESP, or, to be more specific, telepathy. So far, controlled experiments have not been conclusive, but almost everyone knows of well-documented, although admittedly isolated, incidents.

Within my own family, a story is told of a great-great-uncle who was a member of the old Northwest Mounted Police. He was a bachelor and lived with his mother in a northern Ontario town. His job often kept him away for months at a time. One winter, he had been out for about a month covering his huge territory by dog team. As he prepared for sleep in his shelter, he became conscious of his mother's presence, informing him that she had died, but that all was well and he should not grieve. The next morning, because of the impact of this experience, he decided to incorporate an account into his daily professional journal. Many days later, when he reached a telegraph station, a message awaited him; his mother had indeed died suddenly and unexpectedly on that night and approximately at that hour. There is no universally accepted scientific explanation for this phenomenon, nor for countless others like it, but that does not make them any less real. In my own life, I have experienced, and continue to experience, what I believe to be God's call to priesthood. No voices, no images, but a definite urging which, once surrendered to, becomes a daily blessing, as well as a challenge, and certainly defies natural explanation.

I am of the opinion that God's usual way of directly communicating with us is through some form of telepathy which, because it lacks any dramatic features, is often ignored or even unnoticed. Intellect communicating with intellect and nothing between. Such, I believe, is the nature of prayer at its purest level. I suspect that many generations from now, when we are less primitive than we are today, we will regularly communicate with each other over vast distances in the same way. Then our dialogue with God will not seem so esoteric, but will more closely resemble, in terms of mechanics, what will have become everyday inter-human, intercontinental, interstellar communication. But in the meantime, you have every right to suggest that I follow my own advice and put my imagination on hold!

In the Old Testament, God revealed Himself in various sensory and extrasensory ways. He spoke through visions, auditions, dreams and silent interior promptings, as well as through natural elements, such as the pillars of cloud and fire which guided the Chosen People. He told us His name, YAHWEH, meaning "He who is." He makes it clear that He is involved with human history and that to those who recognize His power and submit to His guidance, He is provider of refuge and deliverance. To illustrate this, I offer you a very brief glimpse of some of the highlights of Old Testament revelation history.

In return for taking Him at His word and being obedient to Him, God promised Abraham numerous descendants and possession of a new and rich homeland. This agreement is, in Biblical language, a covenant or a testament. For a time, Abraham's descendants settled in Egypt, where Joseph, Abraham's great-grandson rose from destitution to become second only to the pharaoh. But eventually, Abraham's descendants were enslaved. They became the object of jealous reprisals, for they had grown numerous and powerful, and this led to the famous Exodus which probably took place in the 13th century B.C.

Abraham's descendants were shepherded by a young man named Moses who, although reputedly not a born leader, was called by God who promised, in a spirit of compassion, to assist him. And so we see God, faithful to His promise to Abraham, prepared to rescue His people, to lead them from slavery to freedom. Thus began the march to Palestine, led by an essentially timid man who would find his strength in God. Across the Red Sea, whose tidal waters claimed the last of their Egyptian pursuers, went the nucleus of what would soon become the Hebrew nation.

At length, after failure, pain and effort, the marchers came to the Sinai desert and camped beside a mountain of the same name. Once again God communicated with Moses, and yet another covenant was forged, this time in stone. God called the Hebrew people into nationhood, to be a nation consecrated to Him and bound by His law, and promised them His blessings and protection. Moses served as a mediator between God and His people, preaching God's word to them and praying to God on their behalf when they fell back into their pagan ways. He spoke to them of God's law so recently made manifest in the Ten Commandments. The Ten Commandments dealt with belief in the one God and the people's religious relationship with Him, or as we call it, worship; with the family, and with marriage and the protection of human life; with possessions and their right use; and with justice.

At last, after Moses' death, the kingdom of Judah was established. Over the years, prophets and teachers reminded the people of their sacred historical role; nevertheless, the people fell into the familiar pattern of putting God on the back burner while they pursued, at any cost, the old gods of power and wealth.

In 587 B.C. the Hebrew people were defeated in a war with Babylon, which corresponds, roughly, to modern-day Iraq. The Holy Temple in Jerusalem was destroyed, and once again, the sons and daughters of Abraham faced exile and slavery. And so the scene was set for a new exodus and return to the Promised Land. This happened within fifty years. Persia, now Iran, defeated Babylon and the people of God were free to go home, although under Persian rule. Many years later, the king of Persia lost his crown to the Greeks and eventually, an attempt was made to suppress the Hebrew religion. The result was the famous Macabian Revolt, the outcome of which was blessed freedom for the chosen people. The autonomy they thus regained lasted until Pompey arrived in 63 B.C. and claimed the Promised Land in the name of Rome.

Let us get to the purpose of this brief historical review.

What have we learned about God? Well, to repeat, because it is so important, we have learned that God is involved with man. He did not create us and then turn His back on us. Indeed, He seems obsessed by us, inviting us into a relationship and never giving up on us no matter how quickly and easily we forget.

As we examine God's particular relationship with the Hebrew people, who, as we will eventually see, are our spiritual ancestors, we are struck by how close He seems to be to them, how real, how tangible. I see the followers of Abraham and Moses as little children, being led step by step by a parent who grips their hands very tightly. But, inevitably, as time goes on, although loving no less, parents must let go in order to allow children to grow and become more and more responsible. It is my guess that today we are only beginning to move into our adult years as God's people. Certainly, as confessors, we priests find ourselves with a shrinking rule book, and our penitents accept more and more responsibility for difficult decisions made in good faith with our help and blessing. It is not as easy for either of us. Perhaps that is why there are fewer of us both, but our dignity is surely enhanced.

In the Old Testament, God reveals Himself as being merciful, as being willing to forgive, but not as a wimpy god, for He allows us to suffer for our self-centred attitudes and decisions. And when we are on our knees, aware at last that without Him we are nothing, He offers us, as He did the Hebrew people, once more, His outstretched hand.

But is there another side to this? While God was nursing His Chosen People through one crisis after another, and urging them lovingly toward the Promised Land, as well as toward an ever closer relationship with Him, what was happening to the non-Hebrews? Were the Egyptians, the Babylonians, the Persians all sacrificial pawns, expendable support players? I think not.

God chose to enter into human history in a major way, through what became the Hebrew people. He influenced them and protected them as long as they were true to Him. In this process, there is no evidence of God having done violence to nature, human or otherwise. There were no innocent victims of God's having chosen a specific people to whom and through whom to reveal Himself. Perhaps it could be said that, to a certain extent, because of God's protective hand, those who wantonly attacked or suppressed the Hebrew people had the deck stacked against them, but what is wrong with that? We must remember that when the Hebrews got out of line, they, too soon found out that their God was a god of justice as well as a god of mercy.

God of justice and God of mercy. We have come a long way since our first reflections on an apparent creative force. Before venturing any further, let us retrace our steps and attempt a summary of our progress to date.

He whom we have come to call God has been identified as the ultimate reality, the creator of all that is. He alone holds all things in their state of being. He is omniscient, spiritual and eternal. Although all creation points to Him, He remains perceptible only to the mind and not to the senses, unless He chooses to manifest Himself in an extraordinary way as He did, for example, with the early Israelites, when He proclaimed His guiding presence through cloud and fire.

Man appears to be at the pinnacle of creation, superior to all other creatures, and yet dependent upon them for survival, whether it be the flesh and fruit he eats, or the plant-engendered oxygen he breathes. Thus man, although through intellect and will is the image of his creator, he is called upon to respect, value and, indeed, revere the grass he walks on, the leaves he walks beneath and the animals he walks beside. His responsibility as gardener in the Lord's garden is a great one, so great that without the Lord's help, he cannot hope to succeed. To discern what is good and what is true, and to will and work that the truth be known and goodness done, is mankind's sacred task. Knowing and loving is what we call it. I suspect being human is what God calls it. And so we spend our days and nights somewhere between mother earth and father God, sustained by both.

The fundamental message of the Old Testament of the Bible is that God has revealed Himself to all mankind, both in nature and in history. This leads us to the conclusion that God, our Creator, wants us to find Him, to know Him. Why? Perhaps the answer is somehow linked to the reason He created in the first place.

The Old Testament is a valid historical document. When considering it as a source of revelation, we should ask what it says to our inmost selves, for in the final analysis, each one of us must decide for his or her self. This process, accompanied by the gentle urging of the One who wants us to know, is antecedent to faith.

Abraham is presented to us as a model of faith. Can anyone doubt that he believed? To Abraham and his people, God revealed that He was the Lord. He revealed Himself as being involved in human history. He showed Himself to be compassionate, faithful and just. When He chose the relatively weak and timid Moses to confound the strong, the wise and the arrogant, He demonstrated that His ways are not necessarily our ways. Through Moses, God made a covenant, a contract, with our spiritual ancestors. "I will be your God and you will be my people." When all is said and done, does this mean that the world exists for the sake of humanity? I think so.

Man, regardless of whether or how he evolved physically, remains a particular creation of God. There is no gradual scale of awareness leading up to the human. He was distinct and obviously remains so. Man certainly seems to be God's primary concern; in fact, creation has been described as God's beneficent action towards man. To believe in creation is to believe that God does not depend upon matter, but rather, that all matter depends upon God . . . not just dependED, but dependS. To believe in creation is to see the world as a gift. Beyond this, revelation gives no specific information. How, when, where did life begin? We simply do not know. There is, as we have seen, a point at which the scientists move aside for the theologians. There is also a point at which the theologians step aside for the scientists. We have nothing to fear from a responsible scientific community. We welcome their efforts to uncover nature's secrets, believing as we do that what God uncovers, man happily discovers.

From time to time, we will return to the word and the world of the Old Testament, but the voice of John the Baptizer is now calling to us from the banks of the Jordan River. Like all of the great prophets before him, John has a message to deliver concerning God's involvement with man. It is an urgent message. A page is about to be turned and a new era is about to begin. But before we go any further, it would be helpful, I think, to spend some time in getting to know the religious context within which John's message was delivered, as well as the principal social and political forces at work in his milieu.

For more than a thousand years, ever since the death of Moses, the Jewish people had kept alive, and carefully nurtured, the belief that some day, there would be born to them a great leader under whose rule they would realize all of their corporate dreams, and have the blessing of God and the respect of nations. This future leader was spoken of as the "Messiah," or the "Anointed of God." Throughout those long, hard years, there had been several false alarms, as certain charismatic leaders associated with important political events were hailed by some as being the Messiah. Such stars tended to fall as fast as they rose. But hope never dimmed as God's people reaffirmed their faith in words attributed to a dying Moses: "the Lord thy God will raise up to thee a prophet of thy nation and of thy brethren like unto Me. Him thou shalt hear." These words speak of a successor to Moses in his special role as mediator between God and man. They hint at a new covenant, a new testament, between God and man. These words are echoed by Jeremiah: "Behold the days are coming," says the Lord, "when I will raise up for David a righteous scion."

There must have been a fair measure of despair mixed in with all the hope, as generation after generation failed to produce the promised Saviour. When John stood there, knee-deep in the slow, flowing Jordan, calling the people to repentance, or, as the word suggests, to a rethinking of their values and priorities, the children of Israel had already been under Roman rule for the better part of a century. Understandably, their political and cultural life had reached a low ebb. In their constant struggle for self-respect and identity, they recognized their faith in God as being their principal common bond. They identified themselves as being uniquely "the people of God." They considered themselves to be called to a state of exclusivity and separation. They paid their taxes to Rome and they stepped aside to let the soldiers pass, but they had learned to do so with dignity. Confident in their covenant with God, they looked forward to a culmination of history, when God would triumph over all frustration, humiliation and injustice. And He would do so in the person of His Anointed Prince, who would be of the royal line of David.

How to prepare for the coming of the Messiah was the cause of many scholarly disagreements. Just as today we have our so-called right and left thinkers, our conservatives and our liberals, so too, they had their Sadducees and their Pharisees. The central council of Jerusalem, which reflected the degree of self-rule permitted by the Roman conqueror, was made up of members of both persuasions. On the fringes of the political/religious scene were the Zealots. These people, as their name implies, wanted to see a revolution against Rome. Their dream was of a Messiah who would lead a violent uprising, and who would appreciate having a zealous group of followers who were ready to go into action. At the other extreme were the Herodians. They were quite comfortable with the status quo, which left their puppet king, Herod, with

28

all the trappings of royalty, but precious few of the powers. They were not too comfortable with any talk of a Messiah, because such talk could be considered by the Romans to be subversive. Finally, there were the Essenes. The Essenes were a monastic-like group who lived in the desert and shunned politics in an attempt to purify their religious observance in preparation for the coming of the Messiah.

There was an Essene whose name was John. He lived during the reign of Tiberius Caesar, when Pontius Pilate was governor of Judea. The facts surrounding his life and death have been documented beyond reasonable doubt. He is very important to our search for an authentic understanding of God, because he plays a pivotal role between the two great chapters of Revelation, the Old and New Testaments. And so, turn the page now and we will meet John: John the Baptizer.

Chapter V

John had studied the scriptures with great care and had interpreted them with the purest of motives. He was convinced that the Messiah was already born and was soon to reveal Himself. And so he took leave of his community and set out to prepare the general public to recognize and receive their God-given leader. Curiously, the one whom he would eventually identify and then proclaim as the long-expected Messiah would be Jesus of Nazareth, his cousin, Mary's son, a man of about his own age. Jesus was a gentle, withdrawn carpenter about whom John knew little except for bits and pieces of family gossip, such as the fact that, as a child, Jesus supposedly got lost in Jerusalem and was rather rude to his mother and father when they reprimanded him for frightening them by his absence.

John shared a common messianic expectation of his day, which was that the initial thrust of the Messiah's mission would be characterized by harshness and punishment. "Even now," he cried out, "the axe is laid to the root of the trees, so that any tree that fails to produce good fruit will be cut down and thrown on the fire." The power of his personality and the prophetic tone of his speech convinced many and they asked him how to avoid the vengeance which was soon to come. It is recorded that he told them, in essence, to observe all the demands of the virtue of justice. He demanded repentance, which literally means to reassess one's life in a spirit of humble contrition, and to be open to new patterns of life and new systems of values.

So intense was John and so convincing, that many came to the understandable conclusion that he, himself, was the promised one. At that time, John did not know who the Messiah was, but he did know that it was not himself, and he made this very clear as he prepared for his first encounter with the majestic figure who would come among them to set things right. If someone had taken John to one side and said, "I know who it is. Don't ask me how I know, but I know without a doubt who the Messiah is. It is your cousin, Jesus the carpenter," I like to think that John would have smiled and said, "Try again." On the other hand, had he at the same time been reminded of some of the reverential references to Jesus made by his own mother, Elizabeth, references which at the time seemed to John to be somewhat puzzling, if not bizarre, he may not have found the suggestion entirely ludicrous. Elizabeth had not said much about her own pregnancy or that of Mary, nor had his father, Zacchary, but they had said enough and in such a way as to leave an imprint, a question mark, in a little boy's mind.

One day, John, at his customary place beside the Jordan River, was admonishing his hearers to repent, to prepare for the Messiah who was close at hand. He did not say so, but, in fact, he sensed His physical presence, and quite suddenly focussed on one man at the edge of the group. "There He is," he intoned as though in a trance. All heads turned and, as if controlled by a single impulse, the people made a corridor which found its direction from John's outstretched, pointing hand. Jesus did not hesitate to move forward. What did He do next? Did He take over the meeting, make a quick speech praising John and then bask in the party's endorsement? Far from it. He quietly accepted initiation into the fellowship. He became one of them as He was baptized by a thoroughly perplexed John. Apparently, Jesus did not linger, but continued on His way. Everything happened so quickly that many people realized that something special had occurred only upon observing John's ecstatic expression while he watched his cousin disappear as quickly as He had appeared.

Through his prophetic teaching and lifestyle, John had attracted several close followers, disciples who, from time to time, would leave their work and their families, and, under this inspired teacher, learn the rudiments of prayer and the value of self-denial. They would focus their thoughts on the God revealed in the Old Testament and verbalize the resultant

31

convictions, sentiments and hopes. Sometimes, they would use the words of others and sometimes, their own. They would attempt to deny themselves so as to be open to "the other." Just as Elias of old had built up around his person a school of prophets, so too, John established a school of spirituality that was intended to prepare a select group which would recognize and follow the real Messiah whenever He should appear.

During one such period of instruction and preparation beside John's thatched shelter on the river bank, his students became aware that their mentor had stopped in mid-sentence and was staring intently at a stranger who was approaching from the opposite bank. They, too, looked at Him. He appeared to be just another working man like them, no one very special. Shivers ran down their spines as John stood up, and with eyes aflame, spoke in a voice filled with emotion. "Behold the Lamb of God." As the stranger's features became clearer, Andrew recognized Him as being one who had been baptized only the day before, and he remembered that John had then seemed to be in ecstasy and appeared to be quoting from Isaiah, as the obviously gentle man bowed His head to receive baptism. Yesterday, the stranger had quickly disappeared; this time, however, Andrew decided to follow Him. Obviously, in John's mind, He was someone of significance, perhaps an important link to the long-awaited leader. John did not try to stop Andrew and his young friend, who was also called John, as they got up and left. They easily forded the shallow river and began to walk in the footsteps of the slowly-moving, pensive figure. Unknown to themselves, they had become, at that moment, the first followers of Jesus Christ.

Some months afterwards, John was arrested by Herod's police. In his prison cell, he began to have doubts. On the one hand, he remembered the inexplicably absolute certainty he had experienced when he looked into Jesus' eyes and knew Him to be much more than his cousin. On the other hand,

Jesus was so soft-spoken, so mild-mannered, so unmessianic, that it didn't make sense. John managed to get word to Jesus. "Are you really the one, or should we look for another?" His frustration was surely understandable; he had literally stuck his neck out. No one, not even royalty, had been spared his stern warnings, and now he was in prison, his life in grave danger. If Jesus was the Messiah, then He owed him one. John waited and waited and at last, the answer came back. "The blind see again; the lame walk; lepers are cleansed; the deaf hear; the dead are raised to life; the good news is proclaimed to the poor," and, on a more personal note, "Blessed is the man who does not lose faith in Me." John did not issue a rebuttal. It would seem that he died believing his mission to have been accomplished, for the words Jesus used were familiar to John. They were the words of the prophet, Isaiah, describing the advent of the Messiah. Jesus had, in effect, answered, "I am the One. Look no further."

About two years later, Jesus was dead, executed by the Roman authorities at the request of the Jewish leadership. To many less powerful Jews, the execution of Jesus was a major tragedy. As they saw it, the Jews killing Jesus was like a mother unwittingly killing her own child. Like John before them, they had come to believe that Jesus had been God's most precious gift to His chosen people, the fulfillment of His promise, the Anointed One.

Simon Peter, Andrew's brother, had come to know Jesus very well. He was, perhaps, His closest associate. He was convinced that although, as he said, the rulers had acted in ignorance and, therefore, could not really be blamed, they had indeed killed the author of life whom God subsequently raised from the dead. To this, Peter says, he and his companion, John, are witnesses. Luke, a physician and contemporary of Peter's, records Peter's statement in a written account of the tension-filled days which followed the execution. Peter's words, if taken seriously, were enough to stun any religious Jew. In effect, he was saying: stop looking for the Messiah, He has come, He was among us during the last three years of His life. By a tragic miscarriage of justice, He was executed. Not only was this Jesus the promised and longed-for Messiah, He was, in fact, much, much more than anyone would have dared imagine. He was one with, and equal to, God. Now such a concept was simply beyond imagination, and yet those who believed it spoke with unprecedented conviction, not to mention supernatural power, as many a former incurable invalid was ready to attest.

Try to imagine what it must have been like to be a leader in the Jerusalem community of that time. They thought that the death of Jesus would put an end to their problem. Far from it. If He was a disquieting influence during His lifetime, He seemed to be even more so in death. His followers, who weeks before had slunk around from shadow to shadow, were now standing straight and tall and making the most blasphemous and outlandish statements about God's only Son, an empty tomb, holy spirits and who knows what next. Clearly, all of this had to be stopped now, before the Romans lost patience and came down hard on the leadership, or, worse still, bypassed them altogether and took drastic military action in the streets. And yet, there appeared to be no way of stopping these Jesus people, and their numbers were increasing at an alarming rate.

One of these concerned and frustrated leaders was a man named Paul. Paul was born in Tarsus, a predominantly Greek city in the Roman province of Cilicia, which was close to today's Syrian-Turkish border. Paul was probably about five years younger than Jesus. His family were Jews of high social standing and had been granted Roman citizenship. Paul was, then, a Greek-speaking Roman Jew. Like every other good Orthodox Jew of whatever socioeconomic level, Paul learned a trade, in his case, tent-making, but chances are, he rarely worked at it. He went down to Jerusalem to be educated by the most famous teacher of the day, Rabbi Gamaliel, and in time, he himself became a Rabbi, a doctor of the Law. Paul saw in the followers of Jesus a major threat to traditional Judaism, and he became an ardent persecutor of this growing sect which believed in the resurrection of its leader. A contemporary describes Paul in the following way: "a man little of stature, thin-haired upon the head, crooked in the legs, with eyebrows joining and a nose somewhat hooked." Hardly a flattering description! A comical-looking character it would appear, but a man whose intellectual prowess was legendary. There is no doubt that he was among the most respected of the younger Jewish leaders. So the fact that he, apparently overnight, became an ardent believer of all these wild tales about the carpenter from Galilee was disconcerting to say the least.

The circumstances of Paul's conversion are worth noting. They are recorded in detail by Luke, who takes care to mention that there were several identifiable witnesses. In other words, the story could be easily checked, and you can be certain that it was. Paul, on his way to Damascus to suppress a cell of the new cult, is suddenly thrown from his horse and he hears a voice asking why he is persecuting Him. We are assured that those who were with Paul also heard the voice. The voice, upon being questioned, identifies itself as being that of Jesus. Paul didn't need proof, he was utterly convinced, and history goes on to record his future efforts to convince others.

What, then, can we say of this Jesus, of whom his friend Peter says, "All of the prophets bear witness." Clearly, He was seen by some of his contemporaries as being the Messiah. He was believed to have risen from the dead. He was believed to have been, in some way, one with God, an expression of God, God's revelation of Himself. What had happened during those three years following Andrew and John's decision to go after Him? Why did so many people profess the unbelievable, and do so in the face of terrible punishment and heartbreaking hostility?

Chapter VI

Now it is OUR turn to get to know Jesus, to enter into the Gospels, to make good use of those imaginations we recently put on hold. And at the end, we will again ask ourselves the question, "Is He the Messiah?" and beyond that, "Is He really God?" If so, everything that we have said of Him could then be said of God. What a wealth of knowledge this would represent! What a giant step forward in our quest for God!

Our principal sources will be the combined writings of Luke, Mark, Matthew, John and Paul. All of our source material was familiar to those who lived the actual events, or knew people who did, so we can be sure that there was a thorough screening. This was a subject about which they cared deeply. Remembering and recording it for future generations was a sacred responsibility. The same principle applies to subsequent translations and copies, which were always scrutinized by the believing community in the light of a living tradition, a continuing faith experience.

We return to that day, long before John the Baptizer's arrest, when Andrew and his young companion, John, were moved to follow Jesus, who had been pointed out to them by the Baptizer as being the Lamb of God. It seemed only natural that they should follow the stranger; however, He had not invited them to do so. As they began to overtake Him, they, like young boys approaching a couple of pretty girls at a dance, tried desperately to agree upon an opening line or some other way of getting His attention. They need not have been so concerned. It was Jesus who made the first move. He stopped, turned to face them, and, in a not unfriendly tone, addressed them: "What do you want?" As is so often the case when we have rehearsed an important first meeting, when the magic moment finally arrives, we blow it with something like "How's it going?" One of them answered Him "Where do you live?" Jesus, sensing their awkwardness, smiled, "Come and see." Jesus, like John and his disciples, was camping on the banks of the Jordan. Rough, thatched huts were commonplace and were used by transients. John and Andrew spent the rest of that day in and about such a shelter with Jesus. What did they speak of? There is no record of their conversation. Young John, who was to write a Gospel in his old age, must have considered it to be too personal. Whatever was said, whatever they experienced, they were convinced that John had not made a mistake. This man, Jesus, was like none other. Indeed, He must be the Messiah.

The next day, Andrew sought out Jesus again. With him came, somewhat reluctantly, his younger brother, Simon. Simon, like his brother, was a fisherman, who had left his native Galilee in order to spend some time with John the Baptizer, whose disciple he had become. Simon had a few questions to put to this Jesus. He needed some convincing, in spite of John's endorsement and Andrew's excitement. Simon's and Jesus' eyes locked; the silence was profound. It seemed as if, for a moment, the birds had lost their voices and the river had ceased to flow. Simon's first question died in his throat. He had come to judge, but he knew that the tables were turned; he felt naked, totally exposed, but unafraid. "So," Jesus said, "You are Simon?" Simon nodded. "You will be called Peter." Peter didn't argue.

It was springtime. Jesus had been away from His native Galilee for three months. His little band of followers had grown during the past few weeks. Phillip and Nathaniel had also taken their cue from John, Andrew and Simon Peter and, with their former mentor's blessing, cast their lots with that of the incredibly charismatic carpenter from Nazareth. They were all men of Galilee, and the general consensus was that it was time to go home. For most of them, this meant a three-or four-day walk before they were once more with their wives and children, parents and friends. The journey would be unhurried; they would sleep in fields, buy their food each day, stop at various wells to refresh themselves and hear the latest gossip. Above all, they would get to know each other. And in the evenings, when Jesus, as was His habit, went off to be alone for a while, the five men would exchange their impressions, their reactions, and, especially, their hopes. If Jesus was, in fact, the Messiah, they were very well placed and surely in line for positions of prominence. Even as He prayed for them, Jesus knew what they were thinking. Eventually, they would see more clearly, but not for a long time. God bless them; they were in for many surprises.

They didn't have to go through Cana, but Jesus wanted to do so because He knew that His mother was going to be there for a wedding. In fact, before He had left home, she had suggested that they meet in Cana. Mary was impatient to see her son and to hear of John. Instinctively, she knew that a turning point in John's life, Jesus' life and her own life was imminent. She was uneasy. The road ahead, she knew, was going to be difficult. Joseph's death had only been made bearable by Jesus' presence. She wished He could remain in Nazareth, close to her, but her instincts told her that He was about to begin the long process of self-revelation and nothing would ever be the same again.

The host at Cana welcomed Jesus because He was His mother's son. That He brought with Him some friends was in no way unusual. It would appear that Mary was not a close relative or family friend of either the bride or the groom, because when Jesus found her, she was seated not with the bridal party, but in an outer court, where she could easily observe the frantic coming and going of the servants. As Jesus approached her, He could see that her eyes and ears were tuned to a domestic drama that was unfolding before her. Apparently their host had underestimated the amount of wine required, and the six thirsty newcomers were not about to help the situation. Watching the shrugging of shoulders and the counting of empties, Mary pulled at Jesus' sleeve. "How embarrassing, they are running out of wine!" Jesus' reaction was interesting. He seemed to become upset; not upset over the host's embarrassment, to which He had inadvertently

38

contributed, but upset that His mother should drag Him into the situation. In essence, He said, "Now mother, that is none of our business. Leave it alone." And then, seeing the look in her eyes, He added, clearly agitated, "I am not yet ready." Anyone overhearing would have been hard-pressed to make sense of the dialogue between mother and son, but the two understood each other perfectly well, and He would have been surprised if she had dropped the matter there. For His own reasons, for the sake of continuity, He wanted her to give the word, to make the request which would start Him off in His public life. Mary got the attention of one of the servants and drew him toward Jesus. She said to him, "Do whatever my son tells you." Jesus, in turn, said to the servant, "Take the empty jars and fill them with water, then bring some to the wine steward for his approval." It can be taken for granted that, given the state of agitation of the wine steward, the servant was risking his neck. But he did what Jesus asked. He filled the container and invited the wine steward to sample the contents. Why did he do it? I think that the very force of Jesus' personality, His expression and His tone of voice once again worked their magic, and the servant did His bidding without bothering to ask who He was. But I'm willing to bet that he took a quick taste before approaching his superior.

And so it was that He who would some day take wine and turn it into something far more precious, stepped into the public arena. Apparently, He didn't wait to taste the wine Himself, but, gathering His companions and probably His mother, slipped away.

Before long, it was time to return to Jerusalem, in order to properly celebrate the Passover. Jesus, in company with many Galilean pilgrims, made His way to the Holy City. Jerusalem, as always during the festive season, was bursting, and so were the purses of the merchants who catered to the needs of the visitors. This was especially true of those who operated in and about the Temple, which was the major focal point and the common destination. For the ancient Jew, the Temple of

Jerusalem was God's presence in this world. Synagogues in every city and town were mainly meeting halls for instruction and discussion, but only in the Temple of Jerusalem was God's presence assured. Only in the Temple could sacrifice be offered. Its rebuilding after the exile was the fulfilment of a people's dream. Even today, no place is more sacred to the Orthodox Jew than the ruins of the old Temple and its Wailing Wall.

Deeply conscious of His spiritual roots, Jesus entered the Temple. What He saw made Him very angry. The commercialism revolted Him. The fact that profits and, in the case of the money changers, often huge profits, were to be made at the expense of the poor and unsophisticated demanded immediate action. Reaching down, Jesus picked up some rope ends and waded into the crowd, loudly quoting from scripture and flailing to the right and left. He zeroed in on the money changers' tables, and the proprietors looked on in horror as their neatly piled coins flew in every direction in this madman's wake. Perhaps some of those who accompanied Him, and had been with Him at Cana, looked knowingly at each other and recalled the words of the Psalmist who, in speaking of the future Messiah, had said, "Zeal of thy house has eaten me up." Once again, His authority proved itself irresistible. First, it had been John, who against his own judgement had baptized Jesus. Then, it was the bewildered waiter at Cana. Now, as Jesus cleared the decks in His father's house, no one tried to stop Him. As quickly as it had begun, the scene was over. The merchants got the message and hurried out to find another place to set up shop. And when the dust had finally settled, the Temple authorities came from out of the shadows. "Just who do you think you are?" they asked Him. "Show us your authority to act in such a manner." In reply, Jesus gave them something they could really chew on. Tapping His own breast with what remained of the rope ends and still breathing heavily from His exertion, He glared at them and said, "Destroy this Temple and in three days I will raise it up." The significance of these words was, as yet, hidden from even the closest of His own followers. So, in effect, He gave them no answer; nevertheless, they remembered, and in time they twisted and perverted what He had said and hurled it back in His face at His trial and on Calvary. These people, the religious elite, the scholars, the political leaders, would, with a few exceptions, remain hostile to Him right to the end.

One of the notable exceptions was a leading Pharisee, whose name was Nicodemus. It is quite possible that he witnessed Jesus' angry outburst in the Temple and heard His oblique reference to Himself as being a "Temple," or, in other words, "God's presence." Whatever the case, he was moved by this man, Jesus, and perhaps sought out John or Andrew in order to learn more about Him.

Nicodemus walked swiftly through the city gate and took the road that led to the Mount of Olives. It was a dark night and thus, he hoped, he would be able to pass unrecognized. He had a three-mile walk ahead of him. He was going to the village of Bethany, more specifically, to the house of Lazarus, a well-to-do citizen of that community. He preferred to move in secret, because it was well known that Jesus of Nazareth was staying with Lazarus and his two sisters, and there would be much troublesome talk if it became known that he, the learned and respected Nicodemus, was seeking an interview with the Galilean upstart. Thus, he had forsaken the security and comfort of his own home for the unknown dangers of the night.

Picture the scene that was soon to follow: Lazarus, Martha and Mary, after a polite interlude, left Jesus to sit quietly with the learned Pharisee. The interview was only briefly summarized in John's Gospel, but it probably went on for several hours. It was a discussion of profound mysteries that left a lasting impression on Nicodemus. Little did he know that in about two years, almost to the day, he and his old friend, Joseph of Aramathea, would gently lower this man's tortured body from a blood-soaked cross just a couple of miles from where they now sat. As the dim light of an oil lamp played on their faces, Nicodemus listened intently while Jesus foretold His ultimate giving of self and how, incredibly, His death would result in life. "The Son of man," said Jesus, referring to Himself, "must be lifted up as Moses lifted up the serpent in the desert, so that everyone who believes may have eternal life in Him." The imagery of Moses and the serpent was not wasted on Nicodemus, who was familiar with the event as described in the Book of Numbers. "Moses, in obedience to God's word, made a bronze serpent and mounted it upon a pole, and whenever anyone had been bitten by a serpent, if he looked up at the bronze serpent, he recovered." Nicodemus understood that somehow or other, Jesus, too, was destined to be lifted upon some kind of standard, and that anyone who would meet His gaze with a similar faith would be changed. The thought both chilled and thrilled him as he quietly took his leave and returned to Jerusalem. For him, the world would never be the same. As he made his way home, he pondered over what Jesus had said to him. Jesus had not tried to prove anything; he didn't present arguments as did other teachers; He knew that he spoke the truth and He spoke with an authority that left Nicodemus totally in awe. Nicodemus slowly came to the priceless realization that no matter how we would like to think it, we do not live by reason; rather, we live by authority. It has been well said that reason guides us to the light, but does not give us the light.

Toward the end of that first year, Jesus and his companions were once more heading through Samaria toward Cana. Halfway through Samaria, they came to the village of Sichem, which was the ancestral home of Jacob and Joseph. The village stands in the shadow of Mount Garazin. This mountain was as sacred to the people of Samaria as was the Temple of Jerusalem to the Palestinian Jews. A mile or so outside of Sichem is the Well of Jacob, an ancient and exceptionally deep well which dates back to Old Testament times, and is still in use today. It was to this well that Jesus and His followers came late in the afternoon of the second day of their journey. Jesus suggested that He would wait at the well while the others went into the village to find some food.

He sat there alone, alone in a land whose people were involved in a long and bitter dispute with the people of Judea. Each laid claim to the divinely-appointed centre of worship of the one true God: Jerusalem, with its Temple, and Samaria, with its mountain. Both followed Hebrew traditions revering the same ancient teachers and prophets, but each one had developed its own customs and liturgies, not to mention, prejudices. In fact, the Samaritan challenge to Jerusalem was that of a flea to an elephant, but feelings ran high and Jesus made a mental note to demonstrate to His disciples that they had not cornered the market in goodness. Yes, indeed, there was such a thing as a "good Samaritan." Silently, He loved them, all of them.

She came from the direction of Sichem. She came alone. Most women came to the well in the morning, in groups. It was part of their social life. She came in the afternoon, alone. As she let the bucket drop into the cool depths, she kept her eyes averted from the stranger, who was but an arm's length away from her. Eastern formality and the rift between their people precluded any conversation. She was astonished to hear Him speak to her. She was just preparing to place her water jar back on her head when He asked her for a drink. With eyes still averted, and with a slight tremble to her hand, she passed Him her own cup filled with water: not a sponge soaked in vinegar, but cool, fresh water. The weariness fell from His face, their fingers touched. It was then that their eyes met and she knew that she had nothing to fear from this stranger who had dared to break social convention. She asked Him in a simple and straightforward way why He had lowered Himself in this fashion. The answer she received meant little or nothing to her. It was shrouded in mystery and based upon things not yet revealed. It was, as the late Archbishop Alban Goodier has so beautifully expressed it: "The language of the hungry heart that craved to be known, of the thirsty heart, that craved to be satisfied with the devotion of mankind, simply, that in return it might give to every man no matter what his or her status, the gift of God, the living water."

"You are a Jew and you ask me, a Samaritan, for a drink?" And Jesus answered her, "If only you knew what God is offering and who it is that is asking you for a drink, you would have been the one to ask and He would have given you living water."

Water, living water! Water to her was water, no more. Living water may have meant running water, as in a river, but under the circumstances, He, who didn't even have a cup and needed her help to drink, hardly seemed equipped to improve the local situation. She almost walked away then and there with a shrug and no further comment, but she didn't. She was still curious. "You, sir, have no bucket and the well is deep. How could you get this living water? Are you greater than our father, Jacob?" Jesus did not look up. He poured a little water onto the parched soil; in no time it was soaked up. "Whoever drinks this water will get thirsty again, but anyone who drinks the water that I will give will never thirst again." Then, looking directly at her, He continued, "For the water that I will give will turn into a spring inside you, welling up to eternal life." She was fascinated by the imagery and once more, lowering her burden to the ground, her eyes wide and trusting, she blurted, "Sir, give me some of that water, and then I won't have to come to the well anymore." Jesus did not laugh at her. She had, after all, just made an act of faith in Him.

Now He was ready to open her eyes to who He really was. Would she remain well-disposed, open and trusting, or would she withdraw in the face of possible commitment? What a moment in time! Can't you imagine Jesus, His quiet eyes penetrating her, seeing all and yet remaining easy and familiar? "Go and get your husband and then come back here." She was stunned. She thought within herself that she would not, could not, lie to Him, but neither could she bear to have Him look upon her, as did the villagers, with righteous disgust. Tears threatened, her throat tightened, but she did not give in. With just a touch of arrogance and with her head held a notch higher, she told it as it was. "I have no husband." The divine physician, the model confessor, continued His work. Gently, He helped her to complete her reply. He reminded her that she had had five husbands and that the man she currently lived with was not one of them. Her defence collapsed. "I see, Sir, that you are a prophet." She needed time, time to reflect, time to react. This was too much too fast. And so she tried to change the subject. Pointing to the now-shadowed mountain, she said, "Our fathers worshipped on that mountain, but you people say that Jerusalem is the place where one ought to worship." Jesus noted that she had called Him a prophet and that meant that she both trusted and revered Him. He would lead her toward love and devotion, but, in the meantime, He would follow her in her little diversion and make good use of it. He spoke to her of worshipping in spirit and in truth. She recognized in His words an echo of the prophetic teaching about the coming of the Messiah. Somewhat hesitantly, she spoke. "I know that the Messiah, that is the Christ, is coming and that when He comes, He will tell us everything."

She had called Jesus a prophet; she had listened to His words, even though there was much that she could not understand. She had declared her faith in the coming of the Messiah, as taught by the prophets of old. Now she would be rewarded. Little did she know that in years to come, these moments would stand out as the most memorable of her entire life. Trust and reverence were about to blossom forth into love and devotion. Once again, to describe this moment, which never fails to stir my own emotions, I turn to Archbishop Goodier: "The hungry heart craving to be known, as at Cana, love had compelled it to anticipate its hour and that for a people, as it might seem to us, hardly deserving, so now love compelled it to reveal itself before its time and that to one whom none but Jesus would have thought worthy of such revelation. So explicit a statement we shall not hear again until He stands before His judges, on trial for His life."

And Jesus said to her, "I who am speaking to you, I am He."

Are you beginning to get a feeling for this man, Jesus? A feeling for His personality, His attitudes and His ways? In other words, in spite of the fact that you don't know what He looked like, are you getting to know Him much as you would a well-portrayed character in a novel? I hope so, because that is what these pages are about; getting to know Him by listening to Him and by observing Him interacting with ordinary people from all walks of life, people like ourselves.

* * *

He is a senior official, a member of the ruling class, possibly although not necessarily, a Roman, certainly not a Jew. We are never told his name. His residence is in Capernaum, not far from Cana. He is a man of wealth and power, secure in his position. His future is promising. And then, just when everything seems to be going well, he is rendered helpless and inconsolable. His little boy, his pride and joy, has contracted a severe illness and is clearly growing weaker by the day. The physicians shake their heads. His household, his staff, are full of pity, but can offer no solution. As he goes through the motions of reading and signing dispatches, decrees and requisitions, he pauses over yet another intelligence report, the subject of which is Jesus of Nazareth. Unlike some in his position, this official likes and respects the people over whom destiny has placed him. He is particularly fascinated by their religious beliefs and their messianic expectations. He is also desperate.

Jesus is in Cana. Word soon reaches him that a very important supplicant is on his way from Capernaum. Soon they are face to face. The official explains why he has come. He tries to maintain his dignity by suggesting that if Jesus was as advertised, He could surely cure his son. Indeed, this would be a fine opportunity to establish His credentials. Their eyes lock. Jesus loves this honest, good man, so dignified and yet so close to tears. "Must you see signs and wonders in order to believe?" The thin veneer falls away, as it has with every other open-minded, good-willed person, whether it be a Galilean fisherman, a Samaritan woman or a humble Pharisee. The very force of Jesus' personality has its effect. "Lord, Lord, come to my son before he dies." And then, as though to say, what I do, I do in response to your faith, because I respect and love you, and not to use you to spotlight myself, Jesus says quietly, and to him alone, "Go home, all is well."

* * *

We must not get the impression that Jesus went from triumph to triumph, gaining new followers with every encounter, and blowing away any opposition with a ferocious glare and a devastating verbal thrust. After a number of people had been cured by His word or by His touch, He was indeed sought out by all those who were desperately sick and willing to try anything. Most could not care less who He was or what He had to say. It was what they perceived to be His healing power that drew them to Him. It was this same apparent power that made members of the Sanhedrin, (the Pharisees and Sadducees), nervous and uncomfortable. They put Him under constant surveillance and were often scandalized by what they perceived as His contempt for the sacred. An example of this occurred in the first year of His public life. He was walking through Jerusalem and paused before the pitiful sight of a beggar, whose body was totally ravaged by disease, whose condition was so disgusting as to make him an outcast from even the lowest levels of society. For almost forty years, this vile-smelling, infested derelict had crawled to the same spot each day, hoping to be tossed a few coins which he could exchange for the most meagre of nourishment. The quality of this man's life, if life it can be called, was quite simply beyond our imaginations. We are told that at a word from Jesus, he was cured: the running sores disappeared, the useless limbs filled out and firmed up. He stood. He walked. Before the dazed man could thank Him, Jesus was gone. This episode, one of many of its type, received a good deal of publicity, not from Jesus or his collaborators, but from the Pharisees, whose narrow, encoded vision of religion precluded their sensing the hand of God at work. It caused them to focus upon what, for them, believe it or not, was the central issue: that this restoration to health and the subsequent instruction to the beneficiary to pick up his mat and go home took place on the Sabbath, and was therefore contrary to divine law. It was upon this contravention that the Pharisees focussed. We, however, should not be too quick to judge. In all fairness, the tradition in which these men had been brought up was very rigid with regard to the letter of the law. The law had, in effect, become an end in itself, and its spirit and purpose had almost been forgotten. Jesus took a firm and clear stand when He said that the Sabbath was made for man and not man for the Sabbath. In taking such a position, He made many powerful enemies. For that reason, He chose to spend more and more time in the Galilean countryside, well clear of Jerusalem.

Jesus did not want to be the focal point of a travelling miracle show. Most of the time, He acted out of unadulterated compassion. And in spite of the unsought notoriety that so often followed, He was not out to win a crown; He was not out to gain a fortune nor any kind of power. What, then, did He seek? Look back on what we have already seen; the answer is there. We will find it again and again, as we observe Him and listen to Him.

Jesus decided that it was time to return to Nazareth. Nazareth was very much off the beaten track. It was Jesus' hometown, where He had lived and worked for thirty years. On the Sabbath day, as he walked down the dusty, familiar little street to the synagogue, He was neither greeted as a friend, nor ignored as an unwelcome guest. People He knew

48

by name followed Him, speculating on His purpose, but still keeping their distance. Exchanging Jesus stories had become a major pastime, and now He was back. What would happen next? He had spent the night at His mother's house. There had been no other guests. To most, He appeared to be the same quiet, unassuming Jesus, the young carpenter who generally kept to Himself and had never even married. To some people, He might, for whatever reason, be special, but to most of His fellow Nazarenes, He was simply a little odd but harmless. The stories they had heard did not fit the facts as they knew them.

Like so many others, Jesus had always taken His turn reading and expounding the scriptures in His home synagogue. It was here that the serious young man had attracted the attention of the elders, and they were glad to see Him return. Quietly, He took His seat by the wall. The synagogue began to fill up with more people than had shown up for many a Sabbath. Each person eyed Him as He sat down, expectantly, yet not knowing what to expect. Jesus was invited to the pulpit to read. The scripture to be read on that day was from the writings of the prophet Isaiah. It was not, therefore, a matter of choice; it was handed to Him to be read and commented upon. "The spirit of the Lord is upon me, the Lord has anointed me, He has sent me to preach to the meek, to heal the contrite of heart, to comfort all that mourn."

He sat down. Then He began to speak. He didn't have to raise His voice; the silence was absolute. "This day, in your presence, this scripture is fulfilled."

But all they could see and hear was the carpenter from up the street, nothing more. Jesus told them that He was not surprised by their attitude. No prophet, He said, is accepted in his own country. He compared Himself to Elias and to Elisius, both of whom had been rejected by their own people. The assembly grew furious. He was not seeking their approval; He was turning His back on them. He was calling them losers. Bodily, they lifted Him from His seat and hustled Him out of the synagogue, their synagogue. This arrogant upstart would not put them down and get away with it. Call Himself a prophet? Nonsense! They knew better. It was just as well that good old Joseph had not lived to see the day when his son would show such disrespect and make such outlandish claims for himself! The fulfilment of the scriptures indeed!

In her doorway, Mary saw Him being pushed and thrust down the street and out of the village. The crowd grew in size and anger, and as is so often the case, began to thirst for blood. As they surged out of the village and up the hillside, they became confused and aimless. Finally, in surprise and fear, they began to disperse. Jesus had quite literally disappeared from their midst. Escape had been impossible. That night, there must have been a lot of wine consumed in Nazareth.

Jesus walked toward Capernaum, which would be the hub of His future ministry. How strange, He thought, that in one town they castigate me for curing a sick man on the Sabbath, and in Nazareth, they break every Sabbath rule in the book in their efforts to get rid of me.

In Capernaum, Jesus found friends who would take Him into their homes, but He was, as ever, primarily a man of solitude. Even though a year had passed since the wedding at Cana, He was still not a celebrity in the sense of being followed about by large crowds. That was yet to come. Andrew, Simon Peter and the others who had taken their cue from John and joined Him for a while, had long since gone back to their daily routines. That was not to say that they had abandoned Him, nor He them. A bond had been established between them and they knew that before long they would be together again.

They heard that He was back in their region. His commentaries in the synagogue were attracting attention. People were talking about Him and asking them for details. It seemed to His first companions as they talked things over that He was about to make His move. They decided that it would be best to set their own lives in order, so as to be able to follow Him at a moment's notice, as soon as He revealed Himself.

Very early one morning, they saw from their boat that He was coming for them. They were glad. Whereas a year earlier they had gone after Him, they sensed that this time it would be different, for He was coming after them. And so, instead of instantly running their boat ashore and scrambling onto the beach to greet Him, they waited patiently for Him to make the first move, in what would be a confirmation of their relationship. And so they continued to retrieve their nets hand over hand while, almost surreptitiously, keeping track of Jesus' progress toward them. As the last of their meagre catch slid and flopped into the bottom of the boat along with the last yard of net, they saw that He had reached a spot on the beach not far from them. They looked up. Andrew nodded; Simon Peter waved; Jesus spoke. "Come. Come follow me. I will make you fishers of men." They knew that the moment for which they had been preparing had at last arrived. As they waded ashore, their hearts were too full for speech, for they not only respected this man, Jesus, they had also come to love Him. And so they simply fell into step beside Him as He continued along the beach. Simon Peter and Andrew did not even look back as their crew members grumbled their boat to its moorings.

During the next couple of years, the brothers would return to their business from time to time, but never for very long.

Zebedee had big plans for his two sons, James and John. His was one of the larger fishing operations on the sea of Galilee. Someday it would all be theirs. He was proud of his sons, proud that they would succeed him. Many of his friends envied him his good fortune. When Simon Peter and Andrew approached, he called out to them as old friends. James and John also dropped the nets that they were mending and rose to their feet to greet their fellow fishermen, and introduce their father to Jesus, of whom they had spoken so many times. Jesus did not give them time to speak. He stopped some distance away and beckoned to the two boys, who wasted no time in running to His side. Again, the invitation, "Come and I will make you fishers of men." As he watched them disappear in the direction of Capernaum, Zebedee suddenly felt very old and lonely. He knew his boys well enough not to call them back. His shattered dreams brought tears of resentment to his eyes as he tried to busy himself with his nets. Someday he would understand, but not now.

Chapter VII

Once back in Capernaum, Jesus seemed to shift into high gear. While His four companions watched in awe, He restored to sanity one who had been judged hopelessly insane. According to Jesus, the man was under the influence of hostile spiritual powers. Jesus clearly believed in the existence of a level of creation which, although dependent upon God for existence, was pure spirit; that is to say, knowing, loving, hating creatures who had no material aspect. He called them angels. Some, in their pride, had turned against the God who created them. These, He called devils. And the proudest of the lot, He called Satan. Angels, who in their humility remained loyal to their creator, function in His name as inspirers of mankind, urging us toward good, just as the devils tempt us to do evil and sometimes exert such a degree of influence that God's intervention is required. As I said, Jesus believed all of this. Those who believed themselves to be His intellectual superiors laughed at such nonsense. They still do.

Simon Peter's mother-in-law was also the beneficiary of Jesus' extraordinary powers. At His touch, she recovered immediately from a life-threatening fever. We are told that while still in a state of shock, she thanked Him by preparing dinner for all. The good lady probably never joined them, but bustled about making sure that all she had was at His disposal. I imagine that it was probably a rather silent meal, with each person lost in his own thoughts. Later, the four would talk things over but, somehow, I believe that they soon learned that in Jesus' presence, it was best to remain with their mouths shut and their eyes and ears open. After dinner, Jesus likely went off to be alone. By the time He got back, the house would have been silent and, like the others, He would have soon found a place to lie down and sleep. I wonder whether He dreamed? I doubt that there was time, because the whole household was awakened by sounds of voices out on the now-darkened street. Peter went out to see what was happening. What he saw in the front of his house was every sick and deranged person in Capernaum. Word had certainly spread. Jesus appeared at his shoulder, smiling wearily. He shed a solitary tear which gave silent witness to His concern for miserable people of all ages. There was an eerie silence. Even the sick children stopped crying. Jesus moved from one to the other. A few words, a smile, a touch of the hand, a comforting hug. In every case, it was the same: a new beginning. One man, who was chained like an animal because no one could control him, began to struggle and cry out as Jesus approached. Just before the healing hand shadowed his wild, straining eyes, he choked out these words, as recorded by a witness: "You are the Son of God." The voice of a madman or of one possessed? Insanity or super-human perception?

Jesus, exhausted, returned to His makeshift bed and fell into a deep sleep.

We are told that He made Capernaum His home base, but that He went throughout Galilee, teaching in the synagogues, proclaiming in word and deed the "Kingdom of God." His fame spread, and crowds followed Him everywhere. To some, He was a one-man circus; to others, He was much more.

What was the substance of His teaching? What was this "Kingdom" of which He spoke?

The essence of Jesus' teaching, which we will hear again and again as we continue to accompany Him through His life, was summed up by Him when He said that the most important thing was to love God above all else, and then, to love each other. He said that these imperatives contained His entire teaching.

He spoke frequently of the "Kingdom of Heaven" and the "Kingdom of God." To understand these terms, the full significance of which will be apparent later on, we must be aware that Jesus, unlike some of His fellow Jews, believed in a life after death. He believed and He taught that we were made for not only this temporal life, but also a subsequent eternal life. When He spoke of the "kingdom of God," He was speaking of life as it ought to be lived in preparation for eternity. It is a confusing term, because it is not part of our idiom and we do not seem to have a modern analogy. It signifies, in effect, God's reign, or life under God's rules or guidelines, not a place or a location, but rather, a condition brought about by cooperation between a ruler and his subjects. Obviously, it cannot be lived unless the rules are made known and practicable. Jesus believed that making these rules known was an important aspect of His mission.

Jesus put great stress upon God's love for mankind and upon our consequent responsibility to do our best to come to know and love God. A loving God, although a common enough concept today, was a radical idea in Jesus' time. A powerful God, a mighty God, a just God, yes, but a loving God? A God whom we are to think of as a father? Such a concept constitutes a giant step in our search for God. But it is not a step that we can take with absolute certainty at this stage, because we have only Jesus' word for it, and we have not yet established Jesus' identity or credentials sufficiently to accept His word as being synonymous with truth.

So far, we have observed Jesus to be a man of unique charisma, one who immediately inspires trust and loyalty. We have seen Him to be gentle and caring, yet capable of righteous anger and fearless action. We have observed a man of prayer who needs time to Himself and who seems to enjoy the company of others. We have heard a man who teaches with an authority which leaves no room for error. He never prefaces a statement or a remark with "I think," or "as far as I know." He never asks for advice. Clearly, He has the power to heal and not just in God's name, but in His own. This alone makes Him truly unique in recorded history.

When He speaks of love, which is most of the time, He speaks of the fundamental essence of love, not just a single expression of love, as is so often the case with us. For most of our contemporaries, love is a word associated primarily with sexuality. It speaks of an avid longing arising from a deeply-felt desire for someone, or even something. It is an emotionally charged yearning, which tends to be self-serving. The languages of scripture, mainly Hebrew and Greek, had several words for love, each of which denoted a particular kind or expression of love. They had a word for the above expression of love, but the word used almost exclusively by Jesus, had a very different connotation. First of all, the love of which Jesus spoke is not self-serving; it is very much other-serving. It is placing a high value on someone for their own sake. It is the giving of one's life, right up to and including total self-sacrifice for that someone. The attractiveness or unattractiveness of the person is of absolutely no consequence. It is appreciation and respect, kindness and patience, with absolutely no strings attached. What we are speaking of here, and what Jesus spoke of so often, is fundamental love. It is the yardstick against which all expressions of love must be measured for authenticity. It is the love which Jesus said God has for each one of us. It is the love which Jesus said each one of us ought to have for God and for each other.

The substance of Jesus' message was novel to say the least. Before accepting or rejecting His message, people of His own time, as well as of our time, want to know just who He is and by what authority He speaks. Jesus Himself knew that this was very important and at times, He gauged His progress by asking His disciples who people thought He really was.

So much hinges on whether or not we should give unqualified assent to all that Jesus taught. It is time, then, that we return to His side, as He gradually reveals the nature and source of His authority by what He says and does and by how He says and does it.

Simon Peter, Andrew, James and John spent more and more of their time with Jesus, returning to the lake only periodically to lend a hand with the fishing. Jesus had by now become a famous personality and He was finding it harder to have the time and space to be alone. His teaching was no longer confined to the synagogues. In fact, the entire countryside had become His synagogue. One of the very positive aspects of this turn of events was that fewer people were asking for miracles and more were asking Him to speak and teach.

One day, He was taking what He intended to be a solitary walk along the lakeshore, but word of His presence had spread, and a crowd began to form and press Him from all sides. His only escape route was the lake and, as luck would have it, Peter and his boat were nearby. Jesus sent for Peter, who maneuvered his boat close enough for Jesus to climb aboard. From that vantage point, He spoke to the attentive crowd. He spoke of the "kingdom" in which even now they could participate. He spoke to them of the love which their heavenly Father had for each one of them. He spoke with strength, sincerity and conviction. His love of God and man was contagious. When He had finished and the crowd began to disperse, He asked Peter to go out into deeper water and, of all things, to lower his net for a catch. This was truly bizarre. Peter had fished all night and caught nothing. Clearly, Jesus didn't know what He was talking about; that realization made Peter uncomfortable and, perhaps, a little embarrassed for Jesus' sake. He nodded to his crew, who shrugged and complied. I think Jesus must have been really enjoying Himself. He had serious reasons for what He was about to do, but there is no doubt in my mind that He was going to have fun doing it. As the nets went over the side, Jesus just sat there with a smile on His face. Peter mumbled something about it being a very bright day and frankly wished to himself that he were somewhere else. The men at the oars had faint smiles on their faces too, smiles which quickly turned to concern, as the boat, in spite of their best efforts, began to lose way as the nets drew taut and heavy. Peter gave his orders and slowly the nets were pulled in. It seemed as though every fish in the lake had become entrapped in those straining nets. Gleefully, the crewmen hauled them in, each one calculating the value of his share without giving a thought to how it had all happened. Not Peter. Through his misting eyes, he looked imploringly at the now unsmiling, yet tender, eyes of Jesus. Through his mind there flashed so many different scenes, from John's momentous "Behold the Lamb of God," to his mother-in-law's incredible recovery, to the look on the wine steward's face at Cana. Peter experienced true humility, an overwhelming sense of inadequacy. "Depart from me," he sobbed, "for I am a sinful man." The smile returned to Jesus' face. His arms reached out to embrace the rough and tumble fisherman who had become like a little child. "Fear not, the time has come for you to become a fisher of men." Peter accepted the vocation in his heart and immediately experienced a degree of peace which he would not have believed possible. James, Andrew and John came to assist Peter and his crew with the record catch. With their boats resting gunnel to gunnel, they witnessed what transpired between Peter and Jesus, and they added their silent AMEN, which sealed their vocations forever.

I have always had the impression that Jesus performed many more miracles than He had actually intended. That is to say, more than was necessary in order to establish His credentials as a true servant of the author of nature. Often, He simply responded to human suffering, especially when it manifested itself in the form of physical or mental illness. This explains why He so frequently asked those who benefited from His loving concern to keep it as quiet as possible, at least until He could leave and thereby avoid the hysteria which almost inevitably appeared among the local population, because that hysteria ignored His Gospel message and focused on His ability to perform acts which defied natural explanation. Miraculous power was deemed by Jesus to be extremely potent and to be used only under controlled circumstances. Otherwise, it could do more harm than good. But, it seems that in some cases, many in fact, His head was overruled by His heart. One such case involved a man stricken with leprosy.

To even begin to understand the plight of lepers in Jesus' time, it is necessary to understand the indirect effect upon them of the uncompromising prescripts of the Old Testament book of Leviticus. These prescripts were designed to protect the health of the Jewish people in a natural environment that was often harsh and unforgiving. To be on the safe side, just about anyone with a visible skin condition was apt to be classified as a leper and immediately separated from so-called clean society. Furthermore, these unfortunate people were not generally treated with charity, but rather, with righteous contempt. This contempt was rooted in a complex mental web which linked this disease to sinfulness. And so it was that those designated as lepers bore along with their illness, the projected insecurity of others and all of the harshness that this implies.

One day, in Galilee, Jesus was approached by one of these victims who, with a courage born of desperation, stepped out of his prescribed role and confronted Jesus as a fellow human being in need of healing. Had he kept to the rigid rules of society, he would not have been anywhere near Jesus. Had Jesus complied with those same rules, He would have drawn back from the leper and cursed him for taking such liberties. But neither of the two chose to obey the socio-religious conventions of the day. The leper approached Jesus, and Jesus not only spoke to him, but actually touched him, thereby violating strict ritual prohibitions. By this action, Jesus said a great deal. First of all, He said that He loved and respected this otherwise despised human being. He also said that there can be no law, whether of "church" or of state, which is greater than the law of charity. And most startling of all, He who had turned the water into wine, who had announced to the Samaritan woman at the well, "I am He," whose healing hands had given new hope to so many, said that His words, His power, could literally arrest the dying process in one of its most certain and visible forms. The news of this miracle spread faster than Jesus could move, and before long, He was hemmed in on every side. This was not what He wanted. He knew that this kind of enthusiasm died as quickly as it grew. So He went back to the desert, to pray and be alone. Being alone was a very important part of His life.

What was Jesus looking for? I think that He was looking for those few special people like John, Peter, the Samaritan woman, and Nicodemus, people whose humility, openness and generosity of spirit would allow them to be drawn to Him, and recognize in Him that which they could not yet identify, but which they knew set Him apart from everyone else. He was looking for those who would follow the voice of their hearts on a journey of personal faith in Him, those whose convictions did not depend upon miracles.

When Jesus returned to Capernaum, a number of old acquaintances were waiting for Him. Civil and religious leaders, who had once been content to keep Him out of Jerusalem, thereby ensuring that He could never become influential, had begun to believe that they had made a serious error in judgement. They were now determined to put an end to this interloper once and for all. And so, they gathered in Capernaum, knowing that sooner or later He would return. When He did, they got more than they had bargained for. Seeing them peering at Him from behind every post and archway, recognizing them by their haughty bearing and flowing robes, Jesus prepared to do battle, but, as always, although they may not have realized it, on His own terms. And so He, who had once referred to the temple as His father's house and had swept it clean, decided to really give His adversaries something to get upset about, or, hopefully, something to think about. He would give them their chance, even if He signed His own death warrant in the process.

The scene for the confrontation was set when word went around one day that Jesus was teaching in the main room of one of the larger houses in the town. Several of the Jerusalem contingent hurried to the house in question. They quickly gained entry, for the householder was proud to welcome dignitaries from the big city under his roof. Soon the room was full. The Jerusalem leaders stood there, craning their necks to get a glimpse of Him. Over the shuffling and coughing, they could hear the quiet, measured tones of the master's voice and the voices of occasional questioners.

The poor man was suffering from palsy. Day and night he lay on his mat, shaking and helpless. Those who loved him were determined to take him to Jesus. This might be their last chance. Who could say how long He would be in town this time? Jesus was only a few streets over. It was now or never. They placed the man on a stretcher and carried him out of the house. When they came to the door, they saw immediately that there was no way to penetrate the dense crowd. One of them had an idea, a crazy idea, but one the others agreed, just might work.

In the house, Jesus was replying to a question when suddenly, He looked up and saw, peering at Him through the thatched roof, a face, bearing a very large, very nervous grin. Jesus smiled back. The hole in the roof grew larger. Everyone's attention was drawn to whatever it was that was happening above their heads. The house owner was beginning to use language that would make the proverbial sailor blush. A stretcher poked through the hole. The crowd below fell into a stupefied silence. Hanging vertically from its upper end, the stretcher, with its patient securely lashed on, jerked its way down to a point a few feet away from Jesus. He reached out and helped guide it to a horizontal position, thus eliminating some of the terror from the trembling patient's expression.

In the minds of those who peered down through the hole in the roof, there was no doubt that their friend would be cured. For Jesus, however, events were moving toward a different climax, in the context of which this cure would take on a special significance. Some months before, in the temple, He had incurred the wrath of the leaders because of His reference to "His Father's house." Again, in Nazareth, they wanted to kill Him because of His claim that he was the Messiah. And now, here in Capernaum, He was about to make His boldest claim to date, and to use a miraculous cure as a sign of its authenticity. His smile embraced the sick man. "Be of good heart," he said, "Your sins are forgiven." The patient lay there, still in the shaking grip of his illness. The Pharisees looked at each other in amazement. They had come to pass judgement, to unmask this so-called miracle worker, and now, with the utmost audacity, He was claiming to be much more. Who, they asked, can forgive sins other than God Himself? ? And for once, they had asked the right question. But instead of continuing along the right track, and viewing His words as revelation, they regarded them as a direct and unforgivable insult.

At this point, Jesus was not enjoying Himself. He wanted so much to break through the arrogance, the fear and the pride which blinded these leaders. He did not want to humiliate them; He wanted to humble them. He readily admitted that it was easy to absolve this man of his sins, because there was no way of proving the validity of the absolution. Or was there? Here, in effect, are my credentials, said Jesus, and turning once more to the sick man, He said, "Take up your bed and walk." The man, at least, got the message, because we are told by an eye witness that he left the house whole and well, and praising God. Praising God because he knew that he had been twice touched by the Hand of God. Although this alone would not stand as a proof of Jesus' divinity, it certainly showed Him to be in close, very close, communion with God, and therefore one to be believed.

Jesus never forced Himself upon people, but He always had time for anyone who came to Him: rich, poor, woman, man, child, sick, well, winner or loser. He turned His back on no one. That is why it was possible for a tax collector to become a follower of Jesus: Levi, who made his living by squeezing those who couldn't fight back - Levi, who could call upon the authority of Rome to back him up whenever he chose - Levi, who in spite of all this, was a man with a heart and with a thirst for goodness and truth - Levi, who became Matthew the apostle. The fact that He picked Matthew says a lot about Jesus. But what He did next says, I think, even more. Matthew was so proud to have been identified and selected by Jesus that he called all his friends together and treated them to a sumptuous banquet at which he invited Jesus to be the guest of honour. The banquet was to be held in an open courtyard, where anyone passing by could look in and see what was happening. Matthew's friends were mostly like him: rich, loud and lusty. They were hardly the cream of society. No doubt Peter, Andrew, James and John insisted that Jesus should not be seen in such company, but Jesus took His place at the banquet table. He was not ashamed to be seen with Matthew's friends, indeed, to be seen as one of them. Clearly the party was not according to His style, but if, as is likely, He experienced discomfort, we can be sure that He did not show it.

As we have seen, for those who approached Him in a spirit of humility, Jesus had all the time in the world. It did not matter whether they were ignorant or learned, rich or poor, full of doubt or growing in conviction. But when they came to Him in a spirit of jealous pride, as did so many of the Pharisees, who were determined to discredit Him and thus regain their control of the people, He did not fail to cut them down to size. And so it was that their envy and jealousy turned to hatred, and as their determination to discredit Him was foiled time and again, they began to plot His death. They preferred to find someone else to do their dirty work for them, because public reaction was bound to be strong, perhaps even dangerous. What a coup it would be if they could get their Roman masters to do the job and take the heat. To this end, they began to plot and scheme.

As official animosity grew in intensity, Jesus began to adopt a different teaching technique. He started to make frequent use of parables. These parables were stories which contained a lesson. To His listeners, they often appeared more like riddles, which needed someone with a deeper-than-average understanding of Jesus and His message to explain them. The logical choice for this would be the apostles and other close disciples, to whom we know Jesus gave more complete explanations. Apparently, Jesus was preparing His associates to be teachers. He was, in fact, laying the foundation for an authoritative structure which was yet to be born. By this time, the twelve apostles were never far from Jesus. Andrew, Peter, James and John were still the closest to Him, but He needed the others, too, not only because He had plans for them, but because they gave Him emotional support, friendship and company. The hatred of the Pharisees bothered Him and hurt Him, but what depressed Him most of all was the fact that so few people really related to Him. They flocked to Him in droves, but they had preconceived ideas of what they wanted Him to be. Even His own apostles, much as they loved Him, hardly knew Him. They paraded along the streets basking in His light, perhaps even chancing an insolent glance at the Roman soldiers, as if saying, "Just you wait, you'll soon get yours." And yet, it was a Roman soldier who had been among the very few who sensed who and what Jesus really was. Jesus knew that He would have to spend more and more time with the Twelve, instructing them, strengthening them, expanding their vision, implanting concepts which would be understood only when recalled many months later. Then the day came when Jesus decided that He could send the apostles out on their own. He sent them out in pairs and, to their amazement and pleasure, gave them the power to cure the sick. Imagine their excitement as, for the first time, in Jesus' name, they restored someone's sight or the ability to walk. It must have seemed as if He was working through them, that they were somehow personal extensions of Him, or other Jesuses.

Who could this man be who could multiply Himself in this way and give to others miraculous powers which only God Himself could bestow? Would it be any less strange if the world's finest pianist came up to you or to me and, in a moment, transferred to us his ability to play the piano? Jesus sent his disciples out in pairs, excited, nervous, wondering what they would say when questioned by the learned masters of the law, wondering how they would find the right words to preach Jesus' message of hope and promise. One question which must have been difficult to answer was, "What originally attracted you to this teacher?" They would have had to say, somewhat haltingly no doubt, that He had been attracted to them. Why? They would never know, but that was what had occurred in each and every case. And so, those He chose, He empowered and sent out in His name. He told them to take with them only the barest of essentials, assuring them that their needs would be provided for. They trusted Him. They didn't trust only His intellect and His power, they trusted Him, and because of that personal trust, they accepted His words and His ability to live up to His promises, whether explicit or implicit. With trembling hands, they healed the sick; with dry mouths, they preached the Gospel, often using His own words. He was with them. "God be with you," He had said as they left in pairs, and indeed He was.

Chapter VIII

Sometimes when we Christians read the Gospels, we have a tendency to characterize the Pharisees and the Scribes as having been proud and haughty, powerful and heartless, and generally not too bright. It is probably true that they were an influential body of nitpickers, but in terms of their traditional and perceived responsibilities, this is understandable.

I once asked a famous American Bishop, Fulton Sheen, how he dealt with fame within the context of his priestly vocation, and he told me that he prayed each day for the virtue of humility. In other words, it is not easy to be humble when you are constantly being praised and deferred to.

This was certainly the case with the Scribes and Pharisees, who were held in great esteem, if not awe, by the average person. And they were not stupid; they had among them some of the brightest men of the time. Saul of Tarsus, later St. Paul, was but one example. So when Jesus openly challenged them on matters of both doctrine and practice, He did so knowing that the more He alienated them, the more He would alienate the majority of the people. Jesus did not enjoy having the Scribes and Pharisees as His enemies. He wanted nothing more than to win them over, and indeed, He did have some individual successes, but they were far from the majority. The anger and frustration He experienced in trying to get through to the arrogant leaders are evident in every encounter. Consider, as an example, the time He was asked why He and His disciples sometimes failed to perform the ritual washing before eating, especially when they were in the fields. He answered by pointing out that what made a man unclean "was what came from within, not from without." This is a truism of which we need to be reminded whenever we allow ritual to become empty or detached from the underlying reality. How many Catholics, for example, bless themselves with holy water at the Church door, without so much as giving a thought to their Baptism and its implications? Ritual for the sake of ritual weakens religion. I am reminded of days gone by when a woman would not assist at Mass if she found herself without a hat or veil.

And so, valid though Jesus' position may have been, it was often lost on people whose religious life was dominated by practice and proscription, the origins and intentions of which they did not know. This was a situation with which the leadership was apparently content, but it put a great deal of pressure on Jesus, because it meant that the more He got down to demanding balance, authenticity, reform and openness, the more people turned a deaf ear.

His popularity was draining away. His enemies were sensing an imminent kill. His disciples were becoming more and more apprehensive as they were forced to reassess their expectations.

And so His Galilean ministry began to draw to a close. Ahead lay the long and arduous journey to Jerusalem, which would be the scene of the last days of His public life.

* * *

Jesus was praying, praying to the Father for that handful of men who sat chatting in groups a few yards away. He prayed for them, because He knew that they, too, would suffer in the days to come. He knew that they would experience the acid taste of fear and the gnawing pain of doubt, even despair. He reflected upon the few months that He had spent with them and upon the people and events which they had witnessed, as well as the questions they had asked and the lessons which He hoped they had learned. Peter sat alone, apart from the others. Jesus noticed that he was doing this more and more. It was as it should be. Peter watched Jesus in prayer. It was a sight that always made him feel confident, as he watched Jesus' facial expression gradually shift from anxiety to serenity. Soon he would ask Jesus the secret of His personal prayer life, beg Him to share this source of strength with him and the others. In the meantime, he tried to concentrate on the recitation of his favorite psalms. But watching Jesus at prayer, in total communion with the Father, was in itself a meditation, so Peter gave up trying to pursue his own devotions and just observed his Master. He observed and gradually began to understand. Jesus stirred, rose to His feet, smiled at Peter and walked over to join the others. They were laughing among themselves about the various expressions of shock uttered by some of the Galilean countryfolk who had seen Jesus, that same day, restore sight to a blind man. Jesus listened for a moment and then spoke. He did not need to raise His voice. As someone put another dead branch on the early evening fire, Jesus, looking at no one in particular, asked, "Who do these people say that I am?" Faster than the wine skin which was going around the circle hand to hand, the answers flew at Him: John the Baptist, Elias, one of the prophets. Ironic, thought Jesus; in every case, someone would have had to be raised from the dead. "I see." He said, "and you, you, my closest companions, what do you think?" An embarrassed silence followed. They just did not know what to say.

It was then, over the crackling of the fire and some yards away, that Peter's voice was heard, quivering with emotion. Peter, whose most recent meditation had been Jesus in prayer. "You are the Messiah, the son of the Living God." Even as he spoke, he was amazed at his own words. It was as though their import and their expression had come to him simultaneously.

Jesus silently thanked His heavenly Father for having answered His prayer. The veil was lifting, they were beginning, just beginning, to recognize Him for what He was. We should note here that while Peter did identify Jesus as the long-awaited Messiah, his words should not be interpreted as declaring Him to be divine as well. "Son of the living God" would have been a way of declaring Jesus as being specially chosen by God to be His unique personal representative, as was, for example, Moses. Nonetheless, Peter's clear affirmation of his belief in Jesus as the Messiah caused all eyes to turn to Jesus. What would He say? Would He laugh it off? Would He be angry? In the silence that ensued, each of them reflected upon his personal hope in the national dream which, in turn, centred on the Messiah. Long before, in the times recorded in the Book of Genesis, Jacob had told his sons, "The scepter shall not depart from Judea until He comes to whom it belongs." This was strong medicine for those who were smarting under Roman rule and dreaming of a powerful, free Israel. In the Book of Numbers, Peter and others had read countless times, "A star shall come forth out of Jacob and a scepter shall rise out of Israel." And in second Samuel, "He shall build a house for my name and I will establish the throne of his kingdom forever."

Surely all of this was a promise of world leadership for Israel forever, at least that is what it had come to mean to a people in bondage. Had the time really come? Was Jesus really the anointed one? Was this little band of men to be the first to welcome the long-awaited Messianic Age?

Jesus' response is significant, both for what He says and for what He does not say. He does not deny the title of Messiah, but He does condition His implied acceptance of it in two ways. First, He forbids the disciples to tell anyone; in other words, the statement might well be true, but not in the way it will be understood, not in the popular sense. And secondly, He gives a radical interpretation of what it will mean to be the Messiah. He must endure suffering and rejection, and even violent death. Only through suffering will the Messiah come to glory, a glory which will be made manifest after His resurrection from the dead. Clearly, the popular image of the Saviour or Messiah as being a glorious king, reigning in peace and prosperity, left no room for suffering and death. Therefore, several of the disciples thought to themselves that Jesus could not be the Messiah. And yet, He had not denied it. One thing was clear: Jesus was not about to put a crown upon His head, gather the people about Him and lead a massive revolt against Rome. He did not say, "If you want to be part of what is going to happen, you had better get your swords sharpened and be prepared to ride on to glorious victory." Rather, what He said was "If anyone wants to be a follower of mine, let him renounce himself, take up his cross every day and follow me." Jesus was speaking of other enemies, of other battles, of other victories.

The notion of a suffering Messiah was very hard to accept and impossible to integrate into the framework of general Messianic expectations. Nevertheless, Jesus knew that each time He broached the subject, it was like a hammer hitting a nail a little bit deeper into the resisting, yet yielding minds of His disciples.

A day or two later, Jesus and His disciples were making their way along a secondary path to Capernaum. They avoided the main road, because Jesus wanted to have the chance to be alone with His apostles. As they paused to rest, He told them that He would soon be executed, but that three days later, He would actually come back to life. Mark, who obtained most of his material from Peter, tells us in his Gospel that they made no comment and asked no questions. It appears that they were frightened and confused by His words, so they chose to ignore them, thus entertaining some doubt as to their meaning. For Him to be put to death was nonsensical; He had more than once proved Himself invincible. When the sea had tried to claim Him, did He not subdue the winds and the waves with a mere glance?

They resumed their journey. Jesus dropped behind; only Peter walked silently beside Him, confused and yet content. Among the others, an animated conversation soon began. "I am the most educated," said one; "But I am the eldest," said another; "I have many influential friends," asserted a third. And so the argument went on until they reached Capernaum and the house which they always used, probably Peter's. Once they were settled in, Jesus asked them what they had been arguing about. The question embarrassed them. They did not answer Him, but they knew that He must have overheard them.

They were so unrealistic. All the signs were there. Jesus was on a collision course with the authorities. Sooner or later, they would make a decisive move. He wanted His followers to understand that He was not going to resist, but they, including Peter, were off in fantasy land, dreaming of a kingdom in which Jesus would be the miracle-working king and they the great ones of His court. He was talking about loving service; they were talking about position and power. A little child crossed the room and happily ran to Jesus' outstretched arms. Was the child Peter's? Probably. Jesus spoke. "Before you even begin to understand where I am coming from, you must become like this child." Now, this really deflated them. In the Greco-Roman world in which they lived, a child had absolutely no rights and less status. This was hardly a situation in keeping with the ambitions of those who had been arguing over whom among them would hold the most exalted position in the kingdom to come.

Once again, Jesus was demonstrating that the ways and thoughts of God are not those of man. True greatness, he was saying, means giving yourself in personal service to one from whom you can expect nothing in return, and, most challenging of all, doing so without thinking of yourself as superior. Now that was truly turning things upside down.

One can appreciate that the apostles didn't have it easy. Their traditional concept of the Messiah and His mission was being directly challenged by Jesus, in whose hands they were coming to believe the Messianic sceptre belonged. Their understanding of human success, greatness and worthiness was undergoing radical change. Not unlike some who stumbled through the onslaught of the second Vatican Council, they could not be blamed if they occasionally yearned for the good old days. But growth is disturbing. That will never change. And the apostles grew, as slowly but surely their knowledge and understanding evolved.

Just as the apostles had to gradually purify their concept of the Messiah, so too, they had to develop their knowledge of the God whose representative he was. Peter and his companions were very much aware of how much time Jesus gave to prayer, and it occurred to them that it was the source of His unsettling, but admittedly inspiring, view of things. They wanted very much to better understand Him, so one day they said to Him, "Lord, John taught his followers how to pray, will you teach us?" Jesus' response was immediate. "When you pray," He said, "say 'Our Father' . . . " The rest of the prayer, which has since become second nature to us, was blurred, if not completely lost, to the minds of the apostles, for they never got beyond the word "Father." That one word constituted a revelation of great importance to them and, need I say, to us. The word which Jesus used for "Father" was not the usual formal liturgical term signifying the divine source of all that is. The word He chose was used by children to address their fathers in moments of family warmth and intimacy, and was completely devoid of formality and subservience. Jesus taught them to pray to a concerned, loving God, a patient God, a forgiving God, a God who offers protection to those who are willing to listen: not protection from scraped knees and cold winds, but from false notions and empty values.

As Jesus and His disciples continued along the road to Bethany and Jerusalem, Peter's thoughts returned to Jesus' statement that suffering and death awaited Him. Peter was not only depressed. He was hurt, because when Jesus had brought up the subject again, Peter had tried to comfort Him, to assure Him that no such fate would befall Him. Jesus had lost His temper and had even compared Peter to Satan. It seemed that Jesus wanted to suffer and die. Why? What could He hope to accomplish by allowing Himself to be, like a lamb, led to slaughter? Peter repeated these last words to himself. They sounded familiar. Perhaps the prophet Isaiah? He would have to explore that possible relationship when he had a chance to speak to one of the friendly Pharisees who cautiously associated with Jesus from time to time. No doubt he would see Lazarus in Bethany. Perhaps Lazarus would be able to shed some light on Jesus' determination to sacrifice Himself. Jesus, Peter knew, never gave any indication of seeing a positive value in suffering. He always cured the sick who were brought to Him. He even went to extreme lengths to be sure that those who were attracted to Him did not suffer the pangs of hunger.

Peter's mind went back to the second time that Jesus had used His extraordinary powers to make a little food go a long way. He remembered that the people in the crowd had been mostly Greek, from the area of Decapolis: unlettered peasants adhering to many different religions. Some of them had come over twenty or more miles along rocky paths and dusty roads, but most had come from villages lying within five or six miles from where they had gathered. The harvest was in, so they were free to move about the countryside. A Jewish teacher reputed to have extraordinary powers was in the area. Why not go and listen to Him? And listen to Him they did. For three days they watched Him move about in their midst, addressing them in groups, then quietly walking off to counsel one or another of their acquaintances, perhaps stooping for a moment to pick up a lost, tearful child. The fact that they were not Jews seemed to make no difference. Jesus appeared to love them like brothers and sisters. "Look at them," He had said to Peter. "They must be hungry; their food has long since been exhausted. They have been with me a long time. How much food do we have?" Judas had gone off to see what was available.

Less than a month before, in Galilee, a similar situation had arisen. Jesus had taken what little they had, mostly bread, said a blessing over it and placed it into the hands of the apostles, who somehow managed to distribute it to all present. Strange, thought Peter, the bread multiplied in his hands and the hands of his fellows, rather than through a single dramatic action on the part of Jesus. Suddenly, Peter wished he were out fishing. He always felt this way when he tried to come to grips with the significance of his many fantastic experiences of the last couple of years. Life had been simple before Andrew dragged him into Jesus' presence: simple, but now, seen in retrospect, somehow empty.

The disciples stopped for a meal, forming a circle in a field of stubble by the side of the road. Jesus took a large loaf of bread and began breaking it into chunks, handing one to each of them and calling them by name. "Jesus and bread," thought Peter. Certainly, bread was an important instrument in Jesus' hands. He had used it effectively many times to express unity, concern and brotherhood, not only among His intimates, but among people at large, Jews and foreigners alike. In fact, He had gone so far as to identify Himself, His very essence, with bread.

This happened soon after He first fed the crowd and shortly before the second time. He had made it clear to the leading citizens of Capernaum that they must believe in Him because He had been sent by God. Peter recalled how they had not been antagonistic to His claim, but had wanted more evidence. Jesus was not the first person to perform miracles. What made Him so unique in His relationship with God? After all, Moses had given the people bread from Heaven, moving the psalmist to say that "Men ate the bread of angels." Peter smiled at the memory of the confrontation in Capernaum. It was as though those good people had been setting up a contest between Moses and Jesus. Jesus may very well have pulled off a major miracle by feeding the thousands, but that still falls short of Moses' feeding the Israelites with the manna from Heaven. So if Jesus' claim to be even greater than Moses is to be substantiated, He had better come up with something more convincing. After all, even the prophets were reported to have worked miracles, including raising people from the dead. Peter remembered thinking to himself, "Oh, oh, what will He do now?" But, as he should have known,

Jesus was not one to be caught off guard. The words that had followed continued to ring in Peter's ears. "The bread of God," Jesus had said, "is that which comes down from Heaven and gives life to the world. I am that bread of life. I came down from Heaven so that everyone who sees me and believes in me may have life everlasting."

In the past, when Jesus had spoken along these lines, His listeners, including the apostles, had assumed He was using figures of speech which were beyond their understanding. This time, however, it was very hard not to take Him literally, and this presented very real problems, because, after all, He was still, in spite of everything, Jesus of Nazareth, whose parents were known in the area. In other words, how could He be who He claimed to be when He was most certainly what He was? But Jesus had not let up. Once more, He had spoken clearly and without ambiguity. He had repeated Himself and gone even further. "I am the bread of life. Your fathers ate manna in the desert, but they are dead. I am the living bread from heaven. If anyone eats this bread he shall live forever, and the bread that I will give is my flesh for the life of the world."

Peter once again relived his own reaction to these startling words. Jesus had said them. Somehow they must be true. Even today, Peter could say no more. He saw again in his mind's eye the look of revulsion on the faces of some of the people who had heard Jesus' statement, and heard again one of them asking the obvious question, "How can this man give us His flesh to eat?" Quickly the answer had come: "Unless you eat my flesh and drink my blood, you will not have life in you, but if you do eat my flesh and drink my blood, I will raise you up on the last day and you will possess everlasting life."

For many, if not for most, this had been too much. Jesus had gone too far. Clearly, He was unstable. It was tragic, but it was better to find out now, before it was too late. One after another, they had gotten up, turned their backs on the now silent, watching Jesus and walked out of the synagogue, shaking their heads. He had not called them back, even though among their ranks were some of His most influential disciples. Sadly, He had looked at the twelve who sat as one before Him. As Peter relived the scene, goose bumps rose on his flesh. "Will you also go away?" Jesus had asked. Peter, deep in his reverie, unconsciously spoke aloud the response which had come to his lips on that day. "Lord, to whom shall we go? You are the Messiah."

Peter became aware of the gentle pressure of a hand gripping his arm just above the elbow, and his mind snapped back to the present. Jesus, watching and matching his stride, whispered, so that no one else could hear, "I'll never forget that, no matter what." Peter felt warm all over.

Off to the right, a few hundred yards up the grassy slope stood a shepherd boy. His sheep were scattered about, blending in with the many irregular rock outcrops. Jesus smiled when He saw the boy; both He and Peter waved to him. As the boy returned their friendly gesture, Peter was reminded that Jesus had referred to Himself as a sort of shepherd. Abel had been a shepherd when he was murdered by his brother. Abraham, Isaac and Jacob had all been shepherds. Moses had been a shepherd, as had King David. But Peter had never seen Jesus show anything but passing interest in a flock of sheep, whereas a well-made chair or a nicely-turned table leg never failed to get His professional attention. He had called Himself "the good shepherd." Shepherd of what? Perhaps this was analogous to His statement that the disciples would be fishermen, not of fish, but of men. Yes, clearly that was it; He was a shepherd of men, ready, as He had said, even to lay down His life for them if necessary. Once again, Peter felt the clammy hand grip and encircle His heart. "Please God, no," he prayed. But Peter's heartfelt prayer was interrupted by a deep-throated chuckle. "What are you laughing at?" he asked Jesus. "I am remembering the expression on Zaccheus' face," said Jesus. Peter, too, began to laugh. It really had been funny.

The day before, they had left Jericho later than they had planned, so it was necessary to spend the night somewhere before going on to Jerusalem. They had no definite plans, but many of the wealthy people of both Jericho and Bethany had estates near the road along which they were walking. Some of these people were friends of Jesus, so He was not concerned.

Zaccheus lived on that road in a large, well-furnished home surrounded by fruit trees and flowers. He was a very wealthy man, a senior civil servant employed by the Romans to run the local tax department. He had few friends among his fellow Jews, but he was a realist. He was quite content. Nevertheless, he had been fascinated by the stories he had heard about this man, who was acclaimed by many to be a great prophet, but who numbered a fellow tax collector among his closest followers, and was known to have dined with other tax collectors and their lusty friends. It was even said that he went so far as to tell a story illustrating that the prayer of a Publican could be more pleasing to God than that of a Pharisee. On the strength of that story alone, Zaccheus had begun again to recite some of the prayers of his childhood. The truth of the matter was that he was dying to meet Jesus.

The night before, while on his way home from work, Zaccheus realized that his chance had come. Like everyone else in town, he knew that Jesus was expected, so when he saw the crowd on the road behind him, he stopped to await the parade. Zaccheus was not a tall man and it soon became obvious that if he stayed where he was, he would not even get a glimpse of Jesus. He began to hurry down the road to his own property where some sycamore trees overhung the road. He intended to climb a tree and hide in its dense branches in order to have a good look at Jesus without anyone being the wiser. Within minutes, he was in his hiding place, which, as he had hoped, gave him a good view of the centre of the road. Very soon, the unmistakable figure of Jesus, surrounded by a noisy crowd, and, more closely, by His attentive apostles, began to pass directly under Zaccheus. He held his breath, wide-eyed and motionless. Jesus stopped. He gestured for silence. Was He going to speak? What luck, thought Zaccheus. Suddenly everything went wrong. Jesus looked straight up, directly at Zaccheus and laughed. To make matters worse, so did everyone else, twisting and bending to get a better look at him. Never had Zaccheus been so humiliated. The laughter reached him and froze him to the branches. His face was scarlet. What a fool he had made of himself. Once again, Jesus gestured for silence. Now I am in for it, thought Zaccheus. "Zaccheus," said Jesus in a most friendly tone. 'How does He know my name?' wondered Zaccheus, the bile rising in his throat. "Zaccheus," repeated Jesus, "hurry up and come down, for I am depending upon your hospitality for the night." To hell with the crowd, thought Zaccheus, more excited now than ever before in his life. He scrambled down and raced to open the large, ornate gate which marked the entrance to his property. As Jesus, followed by the twelve, stepped through, the crowd fell silent and Zaccheus' joy was complete.

As is so often the case with good people whose lives are marked with rough edges, Zaccheus' first reaction to Jesus' offer of intimacy was to admit to his failures and vices, and to seek the embrace of pardon and forgiveness through penance and restitution. "Lord," he said, as they walked toward the house, "I promise to give half of my fortune to the poor and to repay any man whom I have wronged." And Jesus gave him the absolution he craved. "This day, salvation has come to this house, for the Son of Man has come to seek and save that which was lost." After that, they all dined well and, over a cup of wine, Jesus told Zaccheus that he would love to have been able to record his expression when he was first exposed in his hiding place. They all laughed and Zaccheus laughed the loudest and longest of all. Less than ten days later, he would dissolve into tears, as word reached him of Jesus' crucifixion.

Chapter IX

I invite you now to pause and do what we have done in the past: reflect briefly upon what we have experienced and observed. It has been said that each one of us re-creates Jesus in his or her own image, and I am inclined to think that this is true. We want to identify with Him, we want to be like Him, or perhaps, more accurately, we want Him to be like us. We stand on the Gospel sidelines, cheering for Jesus and booing those who oppose Him. We are convinced that had we been there, we would have been among His closest and most loyal followers. Perhaps such would have been the case, but I believe that we will never have anything more than a romantic, and therefore, remote, attachment to Jesus until we have the honesty to identify with those who rejected and opposed Him, even with those who crucified Him. In other words, as we realistically identify with the crucifiers, we will be taking a big step toward focussing on the real Jesus. A Jesus created in our own image is one whom we never oppose, but the real Jesus is a constant challenge to our pride, selfishness, greed, lust and hypocrisy, Jesus whose colours we wear, but whose challenge we frequently refuse or dismiss. Who among us can deny that we often consider it more important to be with "it" than with Jesus. On Good Friday, the streets and squares of Jerusalem were packed with people like you and me, people who tended to go with the flow. They joined the mocking chorus, but he loved them nonetheless.

John the Baptizer was the advance man for a Messianic figure whose style and purpose were inaccurately interpreted by almost everyone, including John. John himself was the very image of the prophetic figure whose wild-eyed thunderings drove people to their knees in repentance. Imagine what the Messiah would be like if John was only a foretaste!

"And He came among them as a lamb." "Learn from me for I am meek and humble of heart." "No way," said most of those who had idolized John but, in spite of John's efforts, refused to listen to Jesus. Even John was confused, and he had his doubts about which others must have known. Very few people paid close attention to Jesus, and even after large crowds began to be attracted by His healing power, it remained a fact that very few paid close attention to what He said, or thought about whom or what He might be. To most people, He was "the candy man"; to some, he was a threat to traditional ways and structures; to a few, He was inexplicably unique, respectable and lovable.

Although comforted by the precious few, Jesus was frustrated, saddened and sometimes angered by the others. However, His compassion, understanding and patience dominated His day-to-day activities; to some extent, they even caused the situations which brought Him the most pain. His miracles, for example, which were always precipitated by an immeasurable sense of empathetic concern, were the main reason why He became a kind of celebrity, which, as we have seen, was the last thing He wanted. The pragmatist would have simply decided to refrain from performing any miracles until the people were thoroughly instructed in, and receptive to, his teachings, values and priorities. But Jesus did not function that way. No strategy or plan, however important, ever failed to take second place to the tear-stained cheek of the least of His brothers or sisters. In all of this, He believed Himself to be completely obedient to the will of His heavenly Father, to the God whom you and I are attempting to get to know.

As we walked behind Jesus, through town squares and open country, we sensed how the humble and the suffering were drawn to Him, while the proud and the thriving kept their distance. But the exceptions were frequent and notable: Nicodemus, under cover of darkness, a prominent Pharisee; the Roman official, stiff in bearing, but nevertheless, open and humble; and of course, Zaccheus. Some to whom He freely gave a new lease on life ran off without a word of thanks or a backward glance, but not all. Perhaps some of those who showed little gratitude at first came back later, once they had grown calmer. How happy that would have made Him!

Although the masses did not see beyond the miracles, His chosen companions did. Little by little, they sensed another worldliness in Him. "Lord," wept Peter, soaked and humbled in his half-swamped boat, "Lord, depart from me, for I am a sinful man." It must have been hard not to believe in God when you were with Jesus, and not to believe that His relationship with God was unique. And yet, He remained largely a mystery to His disciples, and like so many of today's Christians, they tended to pick and choose which of His words they would heed and act upon, and which they would, at least for the time being, ignore. Jesus' patience and forbearance were remarkable. Although the disciples stubbornly clung to old Messianic expectations, He gently challenged them to break loose and see and hear him more clearly. "Blessed are the eyes which see the things that you see. Many prophets and kings have desired to see what you see and have not seen them, to hear what you hear, and not heard them." Perhaps His patience with them is partly explained by the fact that He had chosen them; they had not "sold" themselves to Him, convincing Him that they were just what He needed. No, he chose them and told them that he would accept the responsibility for making them what he called "fishers of men." Had they not been chosen, and consequently given all that personal attention, they would have remained part of the crowd, ready to join the bandwagon if it rolled fast enough, but equally ready to yell "Crucify him!" if this was demanded by the winning side. No wonder Jesus spent so much time in prayer. His links with His fellow men and women were so fragile, only His mother was prepared to demand little and give much. She didn't stand in awe of Him, she didn't try to impress Him, she didn't look to Him for reward. She simply loved Him and let Him know that she was doing her best to understand His mission and His destiny. He could talk to her without His words becoming tomorrow's gossip in the streets. With her, He could express fear and frustration, anger and hurt. She was ever the handmaid of the Lord, and in that, Jesus, her son, took great comfort.

As it is with us, so it was with Jesus. Every year seemed to go by faster than the preceding one. But for Jesus, time was particularly precious, for He had only one more week to live. He acted and spoke as though He knew, or at the very least, strongly suspected this to be the case.

It was Passover time and Jerusalem was bursting with pilgrims. Jesus and his apostles found lodgings in Bethany and commuted each day to Jerusalem, where Jesus spent much of His time in and about the Temple, teaching and responding to endless questions. Early in the week, when they had first come from Bethany into Jerusalem, the people had given Jesus an extraordinary welcome. It had been like a victory parade, with the people waving palm fronds like flags. They had welcomed Him as a king to his kingdom. The apostles were not only impressed, they were extremely excited, because they were sure that at last He was to be crowned. But Jesus had not responded as they had hoped and the crowd had soon broken up. Now He made His way into the Temple quietly and without fanfare, but the apostles were still excited. The signs were good. But a couple of days later, in Bethany, Jesus dropped the bomb. "You know," He said, implying that if they didn't it was through no fault of his, "You know, that in two days it will be Passover and I will be arrested and executed." They had hoped that this particular nightmare had been laid to rest, but clearly it was not. What could they say? He did not give them much time, but went on to explain that He needed to be alone. He left them and did not return for two whole days.

Meanwhile, in Jerusalem, "the powers that be" knew that they had to move quickly. Each day they heard more stories about how Jesus had embarrassed this or that Rabbi in front of the people. People were beginning to assume that as He was moving about freely, he must have official approval which, of course, implied some degree of official conversion.

This state of affairs could not be tolerated.

In fact, the situation was not as critical as the chief priests, the Pharisees and their scribes believed it to be. It is true that for the first day or two of the week, feelings ran very high in Jesus' favour, and had He issued a call to arms, the authorities, both Jewish and Roman, might well have been faced with a major uprising. But the people who were ready to risk their lives with and for Him, particularly the Zealots, had instead been told to keep cool. This frustrated and angered them to such an extent that they began to spread word that Jesus was simply not what they had hoped for. He was not up to the ultimate test. So they turned their backs on Him. Many of them began to do some very fast fence-mending with the power structure, lest they find themselves in the midst of a leaderless revolution which had no hope of success. So, just when the chief priests and their allies were beginning to panic, the potential rebels were preparing to cooperate with them in every way, even if that meant crying out "halleluiah!" one day and "crucify him!" a few days later. It was all very understandable, and I for one find it hard to be overly critical of these people. "My kingdom," He had said, "is not of this world." But few had been listening.

Among those who came to the conclusion that Jesus was a loser was a man whose clear and precise powers of reason were never encumbered by emotion, a well-organized, highly-respected man who had little or no time to waste on levity or humor. He perceived love as being an obstacle to the practical management of one's life, so no one could call him "friend," not even those men whose company and whose focus he had shared for the past couple of years. His name was Judas. Like the others, he had been chosen by Jesus and he had said "yes"; he had become the group's business manager and treasurer. He was not an evil man. He was simply given an incredible chance to grow and he refused it. To his way of thinking, humility was to be equated with spinelessness. He disliked Peter and felt Jesus showed poor judgement in grooming him for leadership. He was jealous; he was also greedy, and on this day in Jerusalem, shortly before the Passover, he was one of those who finally turned his back on Jesus and decided to ingratiate himself with the authorities, whose ways and values he better understood.

It was to the advantage of the authorities to take Jesus by surprise, to arrest Him in a relatively remote place, quickly and quietly. Judas would help them. He would win their appreciation and make a little money as well. Why not? He had given Jesus His chance. That night, he joined the others for supper in Bethany. At the same time, Jesus came back from His two days of retreat. It was Wednesday night.

The next morning, Jesus sent Peter and young John into Jerusalem to prepare a place for the group to celebrate the traditional Passover meal together as a family. Judas wondered why he had not been sent, since food purchasing, room rental and the like were among his responsibilities. He was about to ask Jesus to reconsider, when their eyes met and he saw in Jesus' expression a depth of sadness and hurt which told him all and more than he wanted to know. Judas handed the purse to John. John joined Peter, who was already heading for the door, while mumbling the shopping list to himself: "lamb, bitter herbs, bread and wine."

Soon after, according to the strangely detailed set of instructions given by Jesus, Peter and John found a suitable room and set about buying and preparing the food and drink. Later, Jesus and the others joined them; it was to be the last time that they would all be together. All over the Jewish world, similar scenes were taking place: remembering, praying, celebrating, sharing, giving thanks to God. But here, in the upper room of a large Jerusalem home, something more was going on than just the traditional celebration of Passover. Something unique was unfolding. He who was Master, He who always acted with authority, He who people naturally addressed as Lord, got up from the table without warning, and approached the wash stand which stood by the door. His twelve companions watched Him in silence as He took off His outer robe and approached them, a basin and pitcher in His hands and a towel over His arm. Their silence turned to shocked exclamation, as, one by one, He began to wash their feet in the manner of the lowest of slaves. To their protest, He simply replied that He was but giving them an example which they would have to follow, or cease to be associated with Him.

He knew that this would be the most memorable night of their lives. In terms of impact, this had to be prime time. So what lesson, after all these months of training and instruction, did He choose to drive home? "To lead is to serve and to love is to serve, and to permit others to be of service."

Jesus returned to His place at the table and, instead of following the ancient ritual of the Passover ceremony, He shocked His disciples yet again by taking the unleavened bread into His hands, blessing it and distributing it to them, saying, "Take and eat, this is my body which will be given up for you." What was happening? What did this mean? They began to remember and, with each others' encouragement, to tie up previous loose ends. Judas would have been able to put it all together. With his clear and perceptive mind, he would have been among the first to understand that they were witnessing the fulfillment of an incredible promise. But Judas was no longer at table. Moments before Jesus had risen to get the water and basin, Judas had gone off on his final errand. Slowly and with great deliberation, Jesus gave each one of the eleven a portion of the bread. Like children, with wonder and apprehension, they ate the bread. Of one thing there was no doubt: although it looked and tasted like ordinary bread, it was not. His words had assured them of this and they believed Him. How could they do otherwise? Had He not changed water into wine, an event still spoken of in Cana? Had He not more than once given life where before there had been death? Was not Lazarus a walking proof of this? Had He not taken a few loaves of bread and made them into many? Had He not forgiven sins? And had He not given His solemn promise that the bread that He would one day give them would be His flesh for the life of the world? It was happening.

Archbishop Goodier catches the moment with this beautiful commentary: "They heard His words, they knew that they were true. Instantly, they were thinking on another plane, living in another world, a world that transcended human understanding, but was nonetheless true on that account. Nay, it was almost tangible. Faith was more certain than reason. They saw and did not see, but what they did not see was more real than was the object of sight. They understood and did not understand, because human understanding failed them. The impossible was transparently true." I think that this is a priceless description of an act of faith.

Careful as always to take nothing for granted, we should not at this time jump to any further conclusions about the nature and person of Jesus. We are simply trying to experience what the apostles experienced, attempting to grow and advance with them, without having any knowledge or experience of what is to come in the hours and centuries lying ahead.

As would be expected of deeply religious men, they sat, with their eyes on Jesus, speaking in reverent tones, knowing that they were participating in a new and incomparable religious event. They knew that they were making sacred history.

Jesus took the wine vessel and filled His cup. According to custom, He added a little water. As He began to speak again, they fell silent. No one so much as blinked as Jesus, in measured tones, holding the chalice up for all to see, spoke again: "Take this all of you and drink from it, this is the cup of my blood, the blood of the new and everlasting covenant. It will be shed for you and for all so that sins may be forgiven."

Their very purpose for gathering was to celebrate and ratify the covenant made between God and man through

Moses, a covenant sealed with the symbol of life: blood. And now Jesus spoke of a new covenant, a new testament or agreement, sealed not with the blood of a sacrificial animal, but with His own blood. In the minds of the disciples, the words of Exodus ran in parallel to the words just uttered by Jesus: "Then Moses took half of the blood and put it into bowls and the rest he poured upon the altar, and taking the book of the covenant, he read from it in the hearing of the people and they said, 'All things that the Lord has spoken we will do, we will be obedient'. And he took the blood and sprinkled it upon the people and he said, "This is the blood of the covenant which the Lord has made with you concerning all these words."

They were reminded of the prophet Jeremiah, who, generations later, had foretold, "Behold the days shall come," says the Lord, "when I will make a new covenant with the house of Israel. I will forgive them their iniquity and I will remember their sin no more."

As with the bread, the cup was passed to each of the disciples and they drank from it. When Peter tasted the wine, his heart was full. Thank God he had not, like so many others, turned away from Jesus when He first spoke of this common union, this communion. How, the others had asked, with a mixture of disdain and disgust, can this man give us His flesh to eat. How? Peter still could not answer, but he knew nevertheless that Jesus had done it. How? How had He cleansed the leper, restored sight to the blind, calmed the sea? How? It simply didn't matter.

That Jesus had been consciously training and equipping His apostles to share in His ministry was becoming more and more apparent. He had sent them out on their own to preach, to encourage and even to heal. Now, as they sat beside Him for the last time, united to Him as never before, He shared with them His power of priesthood. "Do this," He said, "in memory of me." With this commission, they all became priests of the new covenant. They became the spiritual heirs to those who had offered the ritual sacrifices of the old covenant. Moses' brother, Aaron and his sons had offered the flesh and blood of lambs, which were shared by the people as a sign of their unity as God's people, and of the fact that they lived according to His laws and under His providential care. But now it appeared that Jesus, acting like Moses, in the name of God, was replacing the descendants of Aaron, (the very people who only a few blocks away were making their final plans for His execution), with a whole new order of priests, the first of whom were Simon Peter, James and John, the sons of Zebedee, Andrew, Phillip and Bartholemew, Matthew, Thomas and James, the son of Alpheus, Thadeus, and Simon from Cana. The lamb, the element of sacrifice, was in some incomprehensible way, to be Jesus Himself. Jesus would willingly submit to being sacrificed and, ironically, this act would be performed by the priests of the old law, who would thus unwittingly usher in the sacrifice of the new law. The fruit of that sacrifice would be made available from that time onward, through the hands of the priests of the new covenant. Did the sons of Aaron, Annas, Caiaphas and the others realize what they were doing? No, they did not. Did the apostles gathered together on that Thursday night understand this scenario? No. But all of the elements were there, ready to be put together. And what of Jesus? Whoever and whatever He was, He showed Himself to be at least as significant for His time as Moses had been for his. This much the apostles had grasped: they knew that Jesus believed that He was about to suffer and die, and that, in some mysterious way, His death would not be final. Of course, a lot of uncertainties and unanswered questions remained, and each of them knew that he was involved, intimately involved, in a truly significant evolution. For better or worse, for richer or poorer, they believed that the Messiah had come and that the new order had begun. They were proud and they were humbled. They were joyful and they were apprehensive.

Jesus looked at the men placed about the table. That He had their love and loyalty, He had no doubt. He also knew how unprepared they were for what was to come in a matter of hours. He appreciated that there was nothing He could do or say which would adequately arm them. They would buckle and bend; they would run off and hide; they would deny that they even knew Him. In short, they would panic. Eventually, they would regroup and find unprecedented strength, but first they would discover their own fragility. "Soon," He said "very soon, I will be betrayed and arrested." The chorus was strong and united. "We are with you to the end, even to death. We will never deny you or leave your side." Jesus called for silence. He asked only one thing of them: that no matter what happened to Him or, for that matter, to them, that they never stop believing in Him. Then He continued telling them things which would make sense to them only later. He told them that no matter how much He appeared to be a victim, He was, in fact, fulfilling a destiny which He had accepted from the outset. No one dreaded the next day more than He, but He had a gift to give, and although it was costly, He was going to give it freely and lovingly. That, of course, is the essence of sacrifice, isn't it? To give, at real personal cost, freely and willingly, like the firefighter who scoops up the child from its burning bed, even as his own flesh and lungs cry out for relief. Jesus told the disciples that He was returning to God, from whom He had come, but that He would not leave them alone, for God would be with them and, in some unspecified way, so would He. Through death, He would enter into a new expression of life. They would recognize Him and know beyond a doubt that it was He and that He lived, not as a resuscitated corpse, but according to a new mode of being, which can be sensed only under a special light which He called a Holy Spirit. Only those who possessed this light, this Holy Spirit, would be able to recognize Him. The presence of the Holy Spirit would be experienced more and more completely as time went on.

Pretty mysterious stuff, to say the least, but nevertheless comforting when spoken by Him. The disciples didn't doubt for one moment that He would give them this Holy Spirit, this enlightenment. They had faith in Him and they had faith in the veracity of what He said, not because of internal evidence or logic, but because of their faith in Him.

The realities of which Jesus was speaking were and remain essentially beyond verbal expression, so a point is reached at which human words alone mean very little. As they reclined around the table, listening to His every word, the disciples experienced many dark spots in their comprehension. But such is the nature of faith. It means having enough light to be able to tolerate areas of darkness. Soon they would learn that faith also means remaining faithful in darkness to what one has seen in the light. Faith has so many facets!

After supper, Jesus led the eleven out of the house and beyond the city gates to the garden on the other side of the brook of Cedron. They had passed quiet hours together before in this place, and when Jesus moved off to a secluded part of the garden in order to be alone in prayer, the others were not surprised. His solitude was soon interrupted, as out of the darkness came His betrayer and the temple guard. It had begun. The authorities moved quickly and according to plan. This was Thursday night and they wanted everything to be over by Friday afternoon. The weekend was an important one and Saturday was a special Sabbath which could not be justifiably violated. A specially-convened high court awaited the prisoner, who was accused of blasphemy. Had He not claimed to be greater than Abraham and to have the power to forgive sin? Conviction was assured, but for the death penalty to be imposed, a Roman court would have to acquiesce. And so, early the next morning, the Roman authorities were presented with this now bedraggled prisoner, whose crime had suddenly become sedition. He claimed to be the promised king of the Jews, to be mightier than Caesar. There were many willing to give evidence to this effect.

To the Romans, He was just a Jewish nuisance, and if the Jews themselves wanted Him executed, then so be it, especially since the public seemed to really support the leaders, boisterously clamoring for His death. The condemned prisoner made His way to the place of execution virtually alone. The eleven had scattered, terrified, devastated, confused. The youngest, John, had sought out Jesus' mother, and they, with one or two other women, watched with aching and loving hearts while the sentence of Rome and of the people of Jerusalem was carried out.

It is almost three o'clock in the afternoon. Jesus is remembering: He had finished speaking. The crowd was slowly breaking up into little groups The murmur of a hundred conversations filtered up the hillside. Children who had been hushed by the stern glances of their parents, now gave vent to their energies and raced after each other, laughing and calling. In the distance, the lake sparkled in the bright sun.

Jesus watched the children at play, and his tired face creased into a smile as one of the children beckoned to a friend, urging him: "Let us ask the teacher Himself! Perhaps He will tell us." James and John handed their master a small basket of bread and dried fish and placed the flask of cool wine at His elbow. "We will leave you to your two young friends," they said. Jesus whispered His thanks and turned His attention to the little boy and girl who were standing, uncertain, before Him: "Come, my children, sit down beside me. Are you hungry? Here, have some food. I have plenty for us all." Delighted to be so treated, they crouched down beside Him. The little boy glowed with pride as Jesus placed His arm around his lean shoulders. The girl, his twin sister, not to be outdone, moved in a little closer. And there was an arm for her too.

Jesus forgot His own hunger as He watched His lunch disappear from His lap. Jesus, loving and being loved, was satisfied. "Sir, where do you come from?" "From Nazareth." "Do you like being a teacher?" "Yes; yes, I do." "We heard you teaching the grownups just now, but we couldn't understand. You said that we should not just love our family and friends, but also our . . ." The unmistakable voice of an anxious mother could be heard. "Come children, it's growing dark. We must go home. Come, come quickly. "

In a flash, they were running and skipping down the hill, their question forgotten. A silent blessing followed them, and Jesus was alone.

He is thinking of them now as He tries to draw a tortured breath, longing to wipe away the blood which trickles down over His eyes. Below Him, a blurred fist is shaking, and a rasping voice behind it challenges Him to come down from the cross. Some day, thinks Jesus, perhaps even today, you will know just how easy it would be for me to do just that. And then, if you are humble enough, you'll know why I didn't. But then, perhaps, you will be one of those who will never understand. "OH, HOW I THIRST!"

"Give the poor devil a drink!" sobs the young soldier over on the right. You will understand, thinks Jesus. You will see the light, for you are even now giving me that for which I thirst, LOVE.

"John, John! Take my mother home! She has suffered long enough with me. She understands. She knows that my suffering is the ultimate, the final proof of my love for mankind. What more could I give?

Before it is done, I must suffer every human anguish, pain, fear, loneliness, and yes, even DESPAIR. Only then will my sacrifice be complete."

"MY GOD! MY GOD! WHY HAVE YOU FORSAKEN ME?" His arms, pinned and lifeless, Jesus longs to bless, to embrace, those two little children who sat beside Him on the hillside last spring. They will soon have their question answered.

He had cured their sick, blessed their children, raised their dead, fed them when they were hungry, consoled them when they wept. He had offered them the way, the truth, the life: Himself.

And now, bleeding and twisted, He looks down upon

them. Surely the time had come to curse them, to demand divine justice in all its potent fury! "FATHER FORGIVE THEM, FOR THEY KNOW NOT WHAT THEY DO!"

Poor Peter, hiding with the others, weak and terrified. Soon they will be strong. My strength will flow into them. They will become my hands and my feet. They will follow me.

A few yards away He could see John . . . the only one . . . standing to one side, bewildered and afraid, but still there . . . And beside him, Mary, her face shielded by a thin veil. Seeing her suffering beneath Him brings new anguish to Him. If only she could have been spared this day! And yet, by her presence, by her suffering, she is offering her son to the will of the Father . . . the handmaid of the Lord. She presses her tear-stained face against the apostle's chest. One day, she thinks, it will all make sense, but now! Oh God of Jacob, has He not LOVED enough?

FATHER! The crowd grows silent, expectant. The voice is strong, fresh, vibrant. "INTO YOUR HANDS, I COMMEND MY SPIRIT." His head falls forward. The tense body relaxes and slumps against the bloodstained nails. Jesus is dead.

Thirty years earlier she had tenderly wrapped her infant son in a soft white cloth. And now a full-grown man, his limbs pale with death, is placed before her, cold and empty, His life and warmth completely exhausted. Once more she sees His body wrapped in linen, but this time there is no warm crib waiting . . . only a silent tomb.

Chapter X

And so the time has come to re-examine two questions that we put on hold earlier in this work: was Jesus the Messiah? And is Jesus really God? I believe that the answer to both of these questions is yes, but, what is more important, so did Peter and the handful of men and women who looked to him for leadership.

As we have observed, the conviction that Jesus was indeed the promised Saviour, the Messiah, had been growing for some time, though in a somewhat faltering way, in the minds of the apostles. Their hopes for a military and political messianic leader were slow to die, and, in fact, showed occasional signs of resurgence right up to Calvary and even beyond. But Jesus' persistence and constancy eventually won out. On the fateful night in the garden, when the guards had come to arrest Him, the apostles had seen His face in the flickering light of a dozen torches, composed and serene, never to be defeated. While they tried to melt into the shadows, He turned toward Jerusalem where, as He had said, He would be lifted up and draw all men to Himself, especially the men and women who had shared His life during these past three years, who, in spite of their understandable fear and depression, would not lose faith in Him. Like all of us, who, from time to time, go through the dark night of the soul, the dark night of doubt and aridity, they yearned for the certitude and comfort of earlier days. They learned, as we must learn, that as long as they kept faith, fragile and seemingly insubstantial though it may be, they would know the warmth and brightness of Spring. For them, this would begin on Sunday morning.

They had melted into the night and gone their separate ways, but they wanted to be together, to be with Peter. It is not surprising that they gravitated back to the upper room which held for them so many significant memories. The landlord was a friend, a sympathizer, and he made the room available to them. It was a place of refuge in a hostile city. They spent Saturday in speculation. What they remembered best was that He had pleaded with them to remain faithful, to trust Him, no matter what. Although He had explicitly promised that He would not abandon them, they felt like orphans. He was now sealed in His tomb. A couple of them went out to buy some food and drink. When they came back, Peter thought of doing what Jesus had said to do in memory of Him. He placed the bread and wine on the table, but He went no further. Under the circumstances, to repeat Jesus' words seemed to make no sense. "This is my body!" He was dead! What they needed was life . . . hope. They needed something to celebrate . . . something more than a memory. The meal became like any other except that some of them drank more than they should have. Peter did too. Finally, they drifted off to sleep. It was Saturday night. It had been a joyless Sabbath.

As he laboured to put his mind into gear, Peter was sure of only two things: his headache and the fact that the woman who was trying desperately to tug and talk him into lucidity was not his wife. It was Mary, a devoted follower of the Master, and she came with disturbing news. The tomb was empty. Jesus' body was gone. How, when, why, she did not know, but the tomb had definitely been opened and violated. By this time, John was also awake and the three of them, wrapped in their cloaks, left the room and descended to the empty street, on which the smooth, wet stones were just beginning to reflect the first light of dawn. Within minutes they were standing in front of the empty tomb. Peter was confused. What was going on? Who would have done this . . . and to what end? Peter and John returned to discuss this new turn of events with the other apostles. Mary alone remained at the tomb.

About twenty years later, the apostle, Paul, was writing to the Christians of Corinth. In his letter, he summed up the fundamental elements of the Christian creed as explained to him when he became a Christian, about four or five years after

Peter and John went to the tomb on that first Easter morning. You will see that the focal point of Paul's faith is the resurrection of Jesus, but not 'resurrection' as was commonly understood by those Jews who believed in the resurrection of the dead and an afterlife. Their concept of resurrection was simply the resuscitation of a corpse. The dead person would come back to life and resume his or her natural existence. The resurrection of Jesus as spoken of by Paul is very different. How it differs, and why it was believed in, are questions which we will consider in a moment, but first, we will look at what Paul said to the Corinthians.

This is the earliest testimony to the Resurrection that we have. It predates all of the written gospels and is found in its entirety in the first letter to the Corinthians, chapter 15, verses 3 to 8. In essence, Paul says that Jesus died and was buried and that on the third day He was raised from the dead, that He was seen by Peter, as well as by a number of others, including, last but not least, Paul himself. Paul says nothing about the empty tomb because, in itself, it proved nothing. His faith is based upon Jesus having been seen to be alive after His execution. What does Paul mean by the word 'seen' in this context? You will recall that in his own case, when he was thrown from his horse and heard the voice of Jesus addressing him, he saw nothing, and yet, here he was, twenty years later, maintaining that he was the last to 'see' Jesus. To presume a separate event makes no sense, since it would have been central to Paul's teaching. The answer lies in the way in which Jesus was 'seen' or recognized after his death. Paul's experience and those of Mary of Magdella and the various disciples all point to anything but a 'business as usual' resuscitation of Jesus' corpse, or simply a general experience of Jesus 'living on' through His words and in His followers, like Beethoven through his music and the musicians who reproduce it.

What Paul and the others experienced was unique and not part of our experience. It was intended for a chosen few at a particular moment in history. Consider the general pattern of Jesus' appearances as we read of them in the gospels. Whether in the upper room, the cemetery, on the road or by the lake, Jesus always appeared suddenly and unexpectedly. He was not recognized at first, but when recognition did come, it was certain and needed no further proof. What was there about Him that made Him hard to recognize? Well, to begin with, it simply wasn't the same old Jesus resuscitated. Had it been, His voice and features would have identified Him immediately. In what way did He look and sound different? We do not know, and those who experienced His presence did not seem to think it necessary to go into such detail. Perhaps there was no outward uniformity to the various appearances. Perhaps His face was always in shadow. We will never know, and it does not matter. The fact is that those who knew Him best recognized Him in such a way that there was no room for doubt. Their experience of Jesus after His Resurrection remains distinct from any other Christian experience.

Thus, we come to the meaning of the Ascension; it signified the end of a brief, but vital, chapter in our story. With it the gospels end and the Acts of the Apostles begin. All we have to do is read the opening chapters of the Acts in order to see how encountering Jesus after His death gave back to the apostles their relationship with Him and restored to them their self-confidence. All sorts of theories have been put forth by all sorts of people attempting to explain away, for all sorts of reasons, not so much the empty tomb, but the apostolic experience of the risen Christ. Some have spoken of mass hysteria, others, of outright fraud. As explanations, these may well be less mysterious, but they are also less substantiated, less logical and less believable. Unbelievers have always tried to prove that the Resurrection of Jesus was an elaborate hoax, whereas those who first preached the Resurrection did not seem to be very concerned with proofs. They proclaimed what they believed to be indisputable facts. They were men and women who were convinced beyond question. Of that, there can be no reasonable doubt. Let us go a little further on this same track. Remember we are not trying to prove anything. We are simply attempting to appreciate the experience of those who were the first to proclaim Jesus as risen from the dead. Certainly interesting and I believe, very significant, is the fact that every time He appeared, although their thoughts were probably not far from Him, they failed to recognize Him until He chose to reveal Himself. There He was, standing before Mary Magdalene who was mourning His loss, and she thought Him to be the gardener. And then He called her by name and she knew Him. He called to His disciples from the shore of the lake, and they perceived Him to be a stranger interested in purchasing their catch. Only when He repeated a miracle of days gone by, causing a great many fish to come to their nets, did they recognize Him. And so it was in every case. At a moment of His choosing, their eyes were opened and they knew Him. It is interesting that on more than one occasion, after having been recognized, He ate and drank with them. The empty cup and the remains of a meal were mute testimony to the fact that this was no dream, no hallucination. I think we can conclude that the evidence of the empty tomb did not alone explain their belief. They saw and believed because they were well-disposed, and because He chose to reveal Himself. They did, indeed, see Him with their eyes, but they recognized Him and subsequently proclaimed Him, not because of that visual evidence, but because of an inner certitude which they could not explain, a certitude which equipped them to share so much, but to prove so little. Once again, as at the supper table on Thursday evening, they saw and yet did not see. But what they did not see was more real than was the object of sight. Once again the impossible was transparently true. "It was as though they had within them the ability to perceive realities, the very existence of which transcended but in no way contradicted observation and reason." (A. Goodier)

Needless to say, the belief that Jesus had risen from the dead and that He would therefore continue to live with them in a new and exciting way meant that the apostles would now reconsider and reinterpret everything Jesus had said and done before His death and, in the process, come to some important conclusions. Listen to Peter speaking in those first days, as later recorded in the Acts of the Apostles. Peter stands before the people of Israel and speaks loudly and clearly, without any hint of doubt or fear. He speaks with conviction born of his certain knowledge of the Resurrection, which is, of course, the backdrop for the future four gospels. The Resurrection is, therefore, the keystone, the foundation, the starting point of the Christian tradition. But listen to Peter . . . the NEW Peter. "Let the whole house of Israel know beyond any doubt that God has made both Lord and Messiah, this Jesus whom you crucified. This is the Jesus God raised up and we are His witnesses." And so we have the official proclamation of Jesus as the Messiah.

The notion of a new covenant spoken of by Jesus on Thursday evening involved a new Israel, which would find its unique identity through, and in a personal attachment to, Jesus. Peter and his followers saw themselves as the vanguard of this new Israel. Jews they were and Jews they would remain, but Jews who proclaimed the long-awaited Messiah or Christ in the person of Jesus. They were Jews who would go to the synagogue on Saturdays with friends and neighbours who adamantly rejected the messianic rule of Jesus, then meet again, early on Sunday morning, to do what He said they were to do in His memory. Eventually, the tension between the Christian Jews and the traditional Jews became too great, and the Christians were no longer welcome in the synagogues. And so they began to combine their Sunday observance with the traditional Old Testament readings and prayer forms to which they were accustomed.

Messiah or Christ was not a title cultivated by Jesus during His public life, for reasons which we have already mentioned. But it would not be accurate to say that He refused the title. At His trial, under interrogation, He did acknowledge that He was the 'promised one' of sacred scripture. In order to give it a more seditious ring, this was adjusted by His prosecutors to 'King of the Jews'. The historic bottom line is that had Jesus disavowed the title of Messiah and all of its implications, Pilot would probably not have condemned Him to death. In other words, He was executed for claiming to be the Messiah, a claim, which, as we have seen, had political and even military implications. It was precisely because of this generalized misunderstanding of the Messianic ideal that Jesus, in His public life, had avoided the title, knowing that all His attempts to purify the concept were, for the time being, as effective as 'whistling in the wind'. C.H. Dodd, in his classic work, "The Founder of Christianity" sums it up this way: "Their Messiah is a conqueror; God's Messiah is a servant." I, too, believe that Jesus was, and remains, God's Messiah, the anointed one, who, as He said, came not to be served, but to serve, and to give up His life as a ransom for many.

What did Jesus mean by "giving His life as a ransom for many?" That He 'gave' His life seems to be obvious; He could have defended Himself against the charge of sedition; instead, He chose to let the hastily-woven plot against Him follow its course. Clearly, He was prepared to die for His cause. But what was that cause? He said that it was "the reconciliation of man to God," but we will never understand what that means until we take a giant step in our efforts to identify Jesus Himself.

It is no secret that the common denominator of all Christian doctrine is the divinity of Jesus; that is to say, the fact that Jesus is God NOW and WAS God when He walked the streets of Jerusalem. I am not asking you at this point to accept Jesus' divinity. I am simply stating the fact that the divinity of Christ is a basic Christian doctrine. As a matter of record, it has been my pastoral experience that many professed Christians, Catholics and Protestants alike, are very uncomfortable with Jesus' divinity and tend to reflect very little upon it. I believe that a better understanding of what this teaching means could enrich many people's lives and, needless to say, constitute a major leap forward in our present search for an understanding of God.

Once again we can return to Peter's words: "Let the whole house of Israel know, beyond any doubt, that God has made both Lord and Messiah, this Jesus whom you crucified." The use of the word "Lord" in this context is Peter's affirmation of his belief in Jesus' divinity. 'Lord' and 'Yahweh' were synonymous terms. 'Lord' comes from the Greek translation of the Hebrew word 'Yahweh' or 'God'.

Had someone in the crowd called out to Peter, "Prove that what you are saying is true!", Peter would have had to admit that he could not do so. The divinity of Jesus Christ is simply not a thesis to be proved. No doubt, by this time, you are beginning to realize that most, if not all, major religious truths fall into this category. And so we approach the subject of Jesus' divinity much as we approached that of His being the Messiah.

Jesus never said, "I am God"; much less did He ever say, "I am 'a' god." When we speak of Jesus as being divine, we are in no way suggesting the existence of another god. We have already agreed that there can only be one God, and it is certain that Peter and his fellow Jews, and Jesus Himself for that matter, never questioned the oneness of God. When we speak of Jesus as God, we are speaking of that same God that we began to reach out for on the first page of this book. That is why the understanding and acceptance of Jesus' divine nature has the potential of adding a whole new dimension to our appreciation of God.

Although Jesus did not say that He was God, He did claim to be greater than Moses and all of the prophets. And He did claim the right and power to forgive offenses against God's law, or what we call 'sins'. For this latter claim, He was accused of blasphemy, or of appropriating to Himself the power or office which is God's alone. His accusers were being quite logical as what He said constituted, at the very least, an implicit claim to divine prerogatives. He also said that He was 'One with the Father', thereby asserting that He was the revelation of God. Nevertheless, He never clearly stated that He was God. On more than one occasion, He was referred to and addressed as 'Son of God'. In the idiom of the day, this meant one who enjoyed a special relationship with God, no more, no less. Fifty years later, when the first gospels were put into written form, it is quite likely that the authors attributed much more meaning to 'Son of God' than they did as young men struggling with the implications of Jesus' life, death and resurrection. In their continuing quest for understanding, the apostles no doubt discussed the fact that Jesus referred to Himself most often as 'Son of Man'. Now, at first, this may seem to be a deliberate contradiction of 'Son of God', as though Jesus was trying to 'keep their feet on the ground', while assuring them that His were there too. But in the prophesy of Daniel and elsewhere, the term, "Son of Man," referred to a being who was closely associated with God, although, admittedly, not God himself.

It is then fair to conclude that the titles by which Jesus referred to Himself, and the names which He allowed others to use in addressing Him, do not lead us to any firm conclusions. In fact, most scholars are said to agree that no one recognized Jesus as a divine person during His lifetime. This remained true, even in the first light of His Resurrection and Ascension.

We are compelled to ask: if His closest and most privileged companions, His ordained disciples, could not get beyond the notion of His being the Messiah, how can we who were not even there, conclude that they missed the most significant truth of all: His divinity, His oneness with God? How can we jump to a conclusion which they did not even consider? Our answer comes to us as we go beyond the gospels, to the Acts of the Apostles and the letters of Paul. About a week after Jesus' last post-Resurrection appearance, the apostles, the mother of Jesus and a number of other women experienced together the enlightenment which Jesus had promised. For the first time they understood who and what Jesus was. For the first time, Mary understood that she was more than the mother of the Messiah, she was the mother of Emmanuel: 'God with us'. Peter and the others went out into the streets filled with the desire to share the most important news ever to be announced: the good news, the gospel. Peter stopped people in their tracks. Crowds gathered. They were stunned by, and yet open to, his words. "Let all the house of Israel know most assuredly, that God has made both Lord and Christ, this Jesus whom you crucified." Lord and Christ. That said it all: divine Messiah. Peter and the others believed and proclaimed Jesus to be the Lord of Creation, 'One with the Father', eternal God. Where did this conviction come from? Clearly, it did not come directly from what they had heard and seen. These sights and sounds had conditioned them and made them more receptive to what can only be called a rare and powerful insight, a special gift of God, as Jesus had called it when commenting on Peter's expressed, but barely understood, vision of the truth. "Flesh and blood have not revealed this to you but my Father in heaven." These words prompted Paul to say, a few years later, "No one can say Jesus is Lord, except in the Holy Spirit."

How could pious Jews be led to proclaim Jesus, a man, as God? The very thought of God in human form was blasphemous. Remember these were not Romans who had gods at every turn and a divine emperor in Rome. These were the chosen people of God, a people whose faith in the one God was a sacred trust and the very foundation of their nationhood. Such was their devotion and courage that they would face death rather than even pretend to recognize the divinity of any but the one, true God of Israel . . . the God of Mary . . . the God of Peter . . . the God to whom Jesus prayed. Indeed, Peter's words, the first Christian words spoken, are, when one considers their historical context, a miracle in themselves.

Chapter XI

Although Jesus' divinity cannot be proven in the traditional sense, this does not mean that we cannot place the whole subject of God the Father, the divine Son, Jesus, and their Spirit of light into a context which appeals to our natural taste for intellectual order. What I am trying to say is that, while what we are considering is essentially beyond reason, it is not contrary to it. And so, as we did earlier in this book, we can apply our minds to revealed truth and thus draw many valuable conclusions and progress immeasurably in the quest for God which we began together on the first page of this work.

John was the last to write his account of the gospel of Jesus Christ. He was still in his teens when invited by Jesus to follow Him, and he lived to be a very old man. At some time during the last years of the first century, the Christian leaders of Ephesus asked John to write. John had a special place in Jesus' heart and it was to him that He entrusted the care of Mary, His mother. John agreed to write in order that, in his own words, "You may believe that Jesus is the Christ, the Son of God and, that believing, you might have life in His name." One of the most beautiful and poetic passages in the New Testament is the prologue to John's gospel. In this prologue, John tells us that "in the beginning was the Word." He goes on to say that this Word was, in fact, God. He then tells us that the Word or God was "made flesh," or was, as we would say, "incarnated," and dwelt among us, full of grace and truth. He was the only begotten of the Father. With these key elements of John's prologue before us, and with a sense of wonder and openness in our hearts, we can now move forward.

"In the beginning was the Word." John begins his gospel with the same words that begin the Old Testament: "In the beginning . . . " John is implying that what he has to say has its roots within the essence of God. He is, in effect, re-writing the first line of Holy Scripture. "In the beginning was the Word." What is a 'word'? A 'word' is the expression of a thought or a concept. A thought, an idea or a concept is a good one to the extent that it truly reflects the object represented. For example, I have an idea of an igloo. But that idea is only good and valid to the extent that it reflects the real thing, in this case, an igloo. If my idea of an igloo is of a multilevel brick garage, then my concept is faulty. But it is not totally faulty, because I conceive of an igloo as at least being a structure and to that extent, my idea is correct. Is it possible to have an absolutely perfect concept? What would it be like? Logically, a perfect idea would have to reflect the thing known perfectly and completely in every way. It would mean that the idea would lack absolutely nothing proper to the thing known. It would mean that my idea of an igloo would lack absolutely nothing which is proper to igloos. It would mean that my idea would have to be made of ice and snow. Ridiculous? Of course. But it shows us that an idea is limited by its very nature and can never be perfect in the sense of incorporating everything that is proper to the object. The same is true of the ideas or concepts which we have of ourselves. If it is truly reflective of you, then it is good and valid; otherwise, it is distorted and inaccurate. But one thing is certain, and that is that your idea of self is not absolutely complete and accurate, because to be so, it would have to be everything that you are, including a person in and of itself. So much for your ideas and for mine!

But what of God's ideas? Earlier in the work, we touched on the subject of creation and considered how creation is an act of the will by which something comes into existence. In other words, creation is making something out of nothing and it is by its very nature the exclusive prerogative of God. God's concepts are, then, at the root of all that is; our concepts are but shadows within the same category of being. They are a long way from being perfect, whereas God's concepts are characterized by absolute perfection.

God has a concept or idea of Himself. It is perfect. It lacks absolutely nothing which is proper to God Himself. Consequently, it is a divine being and all of that which is therein implied. It is called "the Word" because it is THE expression of THE Concept. 'It', or rather more properly, "He," is also called "Son" because ideas, like children, are said to be generated. So, too, God, as generator, is known as "Father." Clearly the Son is not the Father, any more than the thought is the thinker. But the Son, being a faithful image, is equal to the Father in every way. And since the Father has always existed, so too with the Son, for the Father has always had an image of Himself.

And now let the drums roll and the trumpets blast as John announces to us that "the 'Word' was made flesh and dwelt amongst us." God became man, one of us, and yet remained still and forever God.

But before we attempt to explore the wealth of meaning in that last sentence, let us back up a bit and return to the Father and the Son before the Incarnation, before that first Christmas. In the Father and the Son, we have, as we have already, I hope, agreed, two beings, two persons. Do we therefore have two Gods? The answer must be "no" because we have already discussed the necessary uniqueness or oneness factor in the very notion of God. We are left, then, with two divine persons but only one God. We have God and His perfect idea of Himself. We do not have God and His clone. We have a being called "God" who is unique in that He has but one nature in answer to the question, "What is He?", but two persons in answer to the question, "Who is He?" Hard to understand? Of course it is! It is impossible to understand! It is a mystery and we are only exploring its surface, using the glimpses afforded us by Jesus and the insights shared with us by saintly men and women. Do not even try to understand. Just remain open to the urging of the spirit as you have been throughout these sometimes arduous pages.

What happens when, figuratively speaking, God the Father and God the Son contemplate each other? This is not intended as a frivolous question. What happens when absolute goodness and perfection reflect upon its own image and vice versa? Perhaps we can find a clue by considering what happens when on our plane, two very dear friends contemplate each other. What is experienced in one way or the other is love . . . an outpouring of self and a mutual acceptance. It is our experience that when two people love each other, they want to give and share. The nature of love is to empty itself. Most of us are too selfish to give unsparingly, so we hold back. We put limits to our loving. There is a point at which we draw the line. It might be our last dollar, or it might be our lives. Most of us do draw the line. But not all of us do so. I am thinking of a young mother in the former Soviet Armenia who, with many others, was buried beneath the debris after a massive earthquake. Alone with her little girl, in a cold, dark pocket within the rubble, after days of utter privation, she cut open her finger in order that her child might drink her blood and possibly gain the strength necessary for survival. This is love. No one has greater love than this. This is emptying oneself in the most literal sense. The fact that they both survived makes this a happy story, but had they not, it still would rate, in my view, as a great love story.

And so, what happens when absolute goodness and perfection reflect upon its own image and vice versa? Love happens; an overwhelming, all consuming love; a mutual, total emptying of self; a love which can be called perfect because nothing whatever is held back. This love is, in fact, God, for God has put Himself into that love totally and absolutely. And so, to the question, "Who is God?" we now add the response, "God is Love." Or as we say, "God is the Holy Spirit." The use of the name, 'spirit', for the third person within the nature of God comes from Jesus having breathed on the apostles while saying, "Receive the Holy Spirit," thus sharing with them, for love of us, His power to forgive sin. The word 'spirit' is derived from 'spiration' or 'breathing'. We can also call upon the image of the 'sigh' as a common expression of love.

What we have been doing in the last few pages is to acquire a deeper appreciation of what is meant by the Blessed Trinity . . . God the Father, Son and Holy Spirit. Many elements of mystery remain, for we are speaking of the inner life of God. But, by virtue of applying our God-given minds to what He, in and through Jesus, has revealed to us, we are able to conclude that the closest we can come to defining God is in terms of knowledge and love. This in itself is a priceless insight. It means we are most Godlike when we are knowing and loving. I am reminded of that beautiful line in the last scene of the stage presentation of "Les Miserables": "To have truly loved another is to have seen the face of God!" This fits well into our understanding of the basis of our human dignity, as revealed in Genesis, where we are told that we alone, of all earthly creation, are created in the image and likeness of God. Now we can say that this means that we are capable of knowing and loving. But what is it that we are intended to know and love? The proper object of Knowledge can be nothing other than truth, and the proper object of love can be nothing other than goodness. Reason and experience tell us this much. For we have all had the unhappy experience of trusting in error and seeking delight in evil. How rich and deserving a subject this is for our meditation. God is knowing and loving. God is truth and goodness.

And now in the name of the Father, Son and Holy Spirit, in the name of truth and goodness, let us return to our consideration of the implications of the Word having been made flesh, so that He, God, might dwell among us as one of us, yet remain still and forever God. As we have seen, the ancient Jews were well aware of the fact that they enjoyed special ties with the one God. Every good Jew accepted Yahweh, the One, the Unknowable, as his Creator, the giver and taker of life itself. He knew that as creature, he must obey and serve the Creator, whose will was made manifest in the Sacred texts. But between God, the infinite, and man, the finite, was a gulf so great that only a chosen few were permitted to even speak the Holy Name.

And then it happened. The Word, the unutterable, became flesh, was made man in the person of Jesus Christ.

It was the greatest moment in history since creation itself and yet, at the time, it was hardly noticed. Even today, after centuries of Christian thought and expression, it remains an event the importance of which has been grasped by very few.

With the Incarnation, the unknown became knowable, the unspeakable became familiar, the fearsome became lovable; God became man. For thirty years there was silence, as though the universe had to rest and reassemble after this momentous happening. And then He appeared among us again ... a full-grown man, one of many and yet apart from all. To look at Him was to look at any man. To be looked upon by Him could mean to be born again. He spoke the language of His birthplace. He wore the clothing common to His neighbours. He ate their food and drank their wine, but He moved about and taught with a surety that spoke of purpose. That purpose would be accomplished at a time and in a manner known only to Him and to His Father, whose perfect image He was. Those who were closest to Him were like ourselves, frequently frustrated by His quiet and deliberate methods. To them, He was like a mighty dam, hoarding its obvious power and releasing only a trickle of water into the parched fields. Even the Baptist showed signs of impatience, and from his prison cell sent messengers to Jesus: "Are you really the One who is to come, or should we look for another?" This message was from the man who had but recently acclaimed Jesus as the Lamb of God, the Messiah, the Promised One who would forever restore Israel, free the people from their earthly oppression and unite them forever to the one God. But He who was so much more than their highest expectations sent back the simplest of messages, which said so much: "Tell John, the lame walk, the blind see, the deaf hear, and blessed is he who is not lacking in confidence in me."

And so He went about His mission: Listen to me. My word is the word of life. Understand my message and you will understand the meaning of life. If you fail to understand, then beware that it is not because of your pride, nor because you do not want to be disturbed. To accept me means to follow me, to love me and to love all that which I love, beginning with the Father and including the most detested and spurned of all mankind. These you must love as I do. Bless them. Feed them. Clothe them. And whenever you do so in my name, you bless, feed and clothe me.

This was the man, Jesus: strong-willed and determined enough to stand up to the powerful Pharisees; tender and compassionate enough to embrace the diseased; old enough to be able to say, "Before Abraham came to be, I am," and yet young enough to die in His early thirties. Such is the eternal Son of the Father; such is God. Know Jesus and you know God. Love Jesus and you love God.

God is, then, the Father, the Son and the Holy Spirit. God is not an "it." He is not a "something," nor is He a "power." God is not a venerable old man with a beard. God is perfect goodness and absolute truth and limitless love. Is God then a person? No. God is not a person in the popular sense, as was emphasized earlier in this work. God is not "an" anything. He cannot be contained within our definitions. When we use the word "person" as in the person called "Father," the person called "Son" and the person called "Holy Spirit," we are simply coming as close to the truth as our language permits, because a being who knows and loves is by our definition a person. That there are three persons in the one nature of God does not mean that God is three people. I'd rather forget about the word "person" in relation to God and simply say that where God is concerned, there are three answers to the question, "Who is He?" As I attempted to demonstrate earlier, this whole confusing business of the Holy Trinity is, in a manner of speaking, the result, the inevitable result, of God's infinite knowledge and love. And so, the troublesome threefold aspect of God follows upon these realities, leaving us to conclude that what is of primary importance is that our God is a God of infinite knowledge and love. This much we can grasp and appreciate. From this major truth flows a theology of the Blessed Trinity, which in turn paves the way for our understanding of the divinity of Jesus: "the Word made flesh."

Chapter XII

Before re-examining the gospels in the new light of Jesus' divinity, it might be useful to briefly summarize what we have already concluded about God. We began by agreeing that any authentic explanation of reality must include a superior creative force. We identified this force as a unique being . . . a rational, purposeful being, who not only is creator in the sense of originator, but also supports in being all that which is. To this being we have given the name God. We came to an appreciation of how God has revealed Himself to mankind, principally, although not exclusively, through the Judeo-Christian scriptures, to which, we conclude, it is reasonable to give assent. From Judaic sources we learned that God is involved with man, that He did not create us and then ignore us. We were able to go so far as to reason that the world exists for the sake of man. Man is the real object of God's love. The Covenant made between God and man through Moses proved that much. God made man His partner in creation; He made man in His own image by endowing him with intellect and will, free will, so that his dignity would not be limited and his gift of self to God and to his fellow man might be true and worthy. It has been said that the created world is the theatre of the power and fidelity of God, because God's supportive, creative action is not just a thing of the past but is still occurring here and now and will continue to occur in time to come. And so, to believe in creation is to see God behind all things and view the world as gift.

In the Old Testament scriptures, God reveals Himself as being both merciful and just. But above all, He presents Himself as being a god who wants to be found . . . to be responded to. And so when all the prophets and holy men and women of Israel had expended themselves for this end, but obtained only minimal results, God played His last card. The Word was made flesh and dwelt amongst us.

Jesus of Nazareth is God. He is God's perfect idea of Himself, expressed in a human being. He is God translated into human terms. He came to teach us how to put "the kingdom" into practice. Or, in other words, how to serve God and each other in a spirit of trust. Jesus will always remain a person of mystery, for He is both God and man. No less God because of His humanity . . . and no less man because of His divinity.

And now let us take a selective look back on Jesus' life, seeing and hearing it with new eyes and ears, for now we know that whatever we see Jesus doing, God is doing, and whatever we hear Him say, God is saying.

As Phillip, Nathaniel, Peter and Andrew set out on that walk to Cana and Galilee so many years ago, their friends probably waved goodbye and called out, "God be with you! " Little did the men know, as they fell into step beside Jesus, that God was, indeed, with them. In Cana, He met His mother and went to the wedding with her. Does it sound bizarre to say that God and His mother went to a wedding? We must never forget that Jesus was fully human. He was not a god in human form, a god masquerading as a mortal. Mary knew Him as her son. She had given birth to Him and nursed Him at her breast; changed His soiled clothing and rocked Him to sleep; answered His questions and taught Him His manners and His prayers. Because of the circumstances of His conception, she knew that He was no ordinary child, but that He was God's perfect idea of Himself, expressed in human nature, was beyond her imagination. In response to her concern and His command, the water became wine. It happened because He loved her and because He understood His host's embarrassment. Does this not bring God down to our level, at least in the sense that we can believe that He actually does relate to us as individuals and takes even our minor discomforts seriously? Jesus taught us that God never has more important things to do, bigger fish to fry. His loving concern is absolutely without limit.

That night when Jesus went off by Himself to pray, as was His habit, did He just talk to Himself? Did He, perhaps, report to the Father, as to the senior partner? Now this may all sound a bit too flippant, but we must admit that such questions are likely to arise. Needless to say, when we try to penetrate the inner life of the Holy Trinity, we must tread lightly. Yet, oddly enough, the potential for humour is very real. The concept of the god-man looks, on the surface, to be the stuff of which humour is made . . . contradiction and incongruity. Perhaps this is because we have not yet even begun to grasp the level of dignity to which our human nature has been raised. When God became man, man did not become God, but, in and through Jesus, came much closer to this than we realize. This happened not so much because of our identifying with Him, but because of His identifying with us. "Whatever you do for the least of mankind, you do for me." In Jesus, then, the human and the divine did not jostle for position, did not at any time contradict each other. Jesus' human nature and divine nature were totally compatible. He was not equipped with a mode switch which enabled Him to function on "divine" or "human" at will. He was all of that which makes a human, human . . . and all of that which makes God, God. Let us not forget, after all, that we, too, are created in the image and likeness of God. We, too, are both finite and infinite, flesh and spirit, at home with time and destined for eternity. But once again, I have gone a little too far. Our eternal destiny can, at this point, only be hinted at. What, then, of Jesus and His prayer? Jesus in prayer was Jesus contemplating absolute goodness and truth, while His stomach ached for food and His feet hurt from walking. Jesus in prayer was Jesus gaining strength from within His own Essence, His own interior life. I am straining for words and images because we can go only so far. Only so much has been unveiled. The rest is mystery. Try as we might, we will never know what it is like to be Jesus. But that shouldn't bother us, because Jesus said that He would never leave us, never abandon us, even in sickness and death. God said that. So we do not need to have a perfect

114

understanding of Him. We only need to know that He has a perfect understanding of us and will not leave us as orphans.

I am reminded of the time when I was flying a small aircraft over the city of Montreal. The Air Traffic Controller asked me whether I could see the jetliner that was approaching from my left. I couldn't see a thing, except a clear sky and a very bright sun. In a somewhat hesitant tone, I said this to the Controller, whose response was cut off by a deep Southern drawl, announcing for anyone on the frequency to hear, "Don't worry, little man, I see you!" Now that is what I imagine God saying to us, as we stumble over the implications of the mysterious union of the two natures in Jesus, wanting to understand, trying to see Him as He really is and often failing. "Don't worry. I see you." That's the bottom line. It's nice to know that even when we do not understand, we are always understood. The question is sometimes asked, did Jesus Himself know that He was God from His earliest years, or did that knowledge come to Him gradually? I don't think that anyone can answer that question, although many have tried. Interesting though it is, I think that question has to be humbly skirted, as we concentrate on what is more clearly revealed. What God wants us to know about Himself is, I believe, much more important than what we want to know about God. Some things may simply be none of our business.

Oh, to have been there that day when God walked into His temple and saw how necessary basic commerce had expanded beyond all proportion, so that the sacred precincts were as a den to thieves who cheated and short-changed those who had come to observe religious custom. What stern judgement awaits ministers of religion who abuse the respect and generosity of those who trust them! "Who are you?" they cried. "Where is your authority?" Remember His answer? "Destroy this temple and in three days I will raise it up." It makes sense now, doesn't it? The temple was seen to represent God's presence among us. In effect, Jesus was saying, "I am God's presence on earth and even though you kill me, I will, three days later, rise again." The significance of His words was not evident at the time, but only later, in retrospect.

One of my favourite gospel stories is the description of Jesus' meeting with the Samaritan woman at the Well of Jacob. There, Jesus demonstrated the fullness and warmth of His humanity. As you recall, the scene was full of tenderness and compassion. He asked the woman for a drink of water. He so much wanted her to be open to Him, in order that He, in turn, might give her more than a simple drink of water. God, wanting to make a friend, wanting to make a friend out of someone rejected by society, ironically enough, in the name of God.

So much was done in God's name; so many rules and regulations became more important than the purpose for which they were originally intended. "The Sabbath," said God, "was made for man," not the other way around. Are things all that different today? I think not. So many of us, clergy and laity alike, place a greater importance on rules and regulations, and on our moral and ethical standards, than we do on people who often feel burdened by them. This does not mean that standards are not necessary. They are, but only in the context of charity and respect. We turn away so many people, young and old, when they need us most. Jesus never did that. God does not do that. That is the way of the scribes and Pharisees, both then and now.

Much of the publicity surrounding Jesus' life focussed on His miracles. If Jesus was so moved by human pain and illness that He never refused to cure an afflicted person, why does He, God, permit these things in the first place? I guess this is as good a time as any to address the problem of evil in God's created universe. Why illness? Why earthquakes? Why man's inhumanity to man? And his denial of God?

I don't think that there is a simple answer to any of these questions. We all experience the perversity of human nature. Greed and selfishness seem to exist as a direct consequence of man's freedom to be generous and selfless. This freedom is very important to our dignity. It defines us. Without it, we could not be good. We could not give. Unfortunately, that same freedom also enables us to be evil and do violence. The only cure for this, it seems to me, is for God to deprive us of our free will and lock us into some kind of defined focus on the "good." But then, we would cease to be in His image and thus, we would cease to be human.

Nature, too, can be perverse. The waters which carry and sustain us in many ways may combine with the winds, borne of our life-giving sun, to produce merciless killer storms. The very material of which our planet and its life-supporting fuels and plants is constituted can boil and churn and strain and slip to produce volcanic eruptions, landslides and earthquakes.

Are not all of these forces subject to the same basic law, which says that everything having potential for good also has potential for harm? Fire can burn, water can destroy, gravity can crush. Can you imagine a world in which water could not drown, or otherwise damage, fire could not burn, flesh could not decay, bones could not break, blood could not spill, a brain could not malfunction, and eyes could not be blinded? I am unable to imagine such a world, unless, of course, I call it Heaven, and then it is no longer "this" world. The proverbial bottom line is that creation is not perfect. God alone is perfect. As far as humanity is concerned, we know that we all have an insatiable thirst for happiness. But we also know that, by definition, complete and lasting happiness is found only in perfection and therefore, cannot be found in this world. Perhaps, then, humanity is designed not only for this world, but for another as well, in which this universal appetite will, at long last, be satisfied. If not, then human kind is the victim of a cruel trick. But a trick perpetrated by whom? Surely not God. Not the God that we are getting to know.

In spite of the apparent fickleness of a material universe, in which the elements and forces not only nourish and support us, but also starve and destroy us, most of our sorrows can be lessened and made more bearable by human concern and kindness. These two qualities were ever present in Jesus' day-to-day interaction with people of every level of society. We are reminded of the miraculous cures effected by Jesus. Clearly He wanted His followers to always show the utmost concern for those who were crippled, diseased, malnourished or otherwise hurting. Obviously, He didn't believe that being sick or hungry was a good thing; if He had, He would have left suffering people as they were. God wants us to fight hunger and disease wherever we find it. If people are sick and hungry because of our neglect, then we are failing God. We are failing as His reflections. We are failing as human beings.

I well remember an incident, many years ago, during the frightful famine in Ethiopia, when a priest who was living there was asked by a shocked and shaken television reporter, "Father, don't you look around you and sometimes ask, Where is God?" "No," replied the priest, "but every day I ask, where is man?"

If saying, on the one hand, that God is the author of nature, and on the other, that He wants us to fight the negative effects of His imperfect creation seems to be contradictory, let me respond again that God clearly intended to create an imperfect universe. Why? Because, on balance, it is the best environment for us to function in, to achieve our full potential. Remember, creation is for man and man is for God.

Continuing in the same vein, I would like to share with you a view of life which colours my understanding of much of what I see and experience. I believe that there exists a continuing struggle between truth and goodness on one side, and power and wealth on the other. Now, I do not see this struggle in terms as clear-cut and simple as good versus evil, or right versus wrong. The scene that I am watching and in which I am also a participant is far more fluid than that, and far less defined. First of all, I believe that there is nothing inherently wrong with either wealth or power. I am, however, convinced that both of these states should always be subordinated to truth and goodness. When Jesus contrasted the children of this world with the children of light, He was not condemning one group and blessing the other, because, in reality, there is a single family of man, most of whose members tend to move about in varying degrees of shade.

But when power and wealth are pursued at any cost, without reference to truth and goodness, we have the basic recipe for war, civil strife, injustice, dehumanizing poverty of the many and equally dehumanizing wealth of the few.

Often, this unconscionable pursuit of wealth and power is given another guise, which serves to mask it. For example, when in a certain region the economic pie is not very large, people tend to group according to religion, ethnic background or colour of skin, in order to establish a relatively small elite, which attempts to terrorize others into withdrawing from the political and economic contest. What is happening is not Protestants fighting Catholics, or whites fighting blacks, but rather, people struggling for wealth and power.

At the present time, people's appetites for wealth and power are whetted as never before. Most advertising, by its very nature, encourages excessive consumerism, which, of course, demands that more and more wealth be placed into the hands of the individual, whose primary goal then becomes the acquisition of goods at whatever cost. It is the "at whatever cost" factor that presents the problem, as this leads to the destruction of balance between the truth and goodness forces and those of wealth and power. We are dealing here, in a sense, with competing gods: the God who is goodness and truth and the god who is power and wealth. Jesus identified this contest and said quite simply that one cannot serve both as masters. However, a person can be both wealthy and powerful and remain faithful to the one true God, who is the essence of truth and goodness. It comes down to a question of how and why one acquires that power and wealth and what one does with it. It is obvious that achieving this balance and maintaining it is not easy. Jesus Himself said that the challenges faced by the rich were very real and the pitfalls many.

I believe that the more a society canonizes wealth and power, the less likely are those most vulnerable to influence, our youth, likely to see any validity in, or need for, religion. The more affluent the society and the more crowded the stores, the emptier the churches. It need not be that way, but it usually is, even on Sundays!

Such are the risks inherent in our dignity. We are free men and women created in God's image and thereby, blessed with intellect and will. Intellect and will have as their proper objects truth and goodness or, ultimately, God Himself, whose principal activity is, in our terms, reduced to knowing and loving. Nevertheless, we can choose and choose we do . . . every day and every hour. Sometimes, we fail to perceive what is good or what is true. This is ignorance, one of the things that makes us less than God. Sometimes, our perception is accurate, but our choice is dictated solely by the demands of wealth or power in some shape or form. This is sin and it drives a wedge between ourselves and God. It tends to be habit-forming and it becomes easier with repetition.

And so we stand on this unsteady planet, proving ourselves as we cope with it, with each other and above all, with ourselves. Yes, there are such realities as ignorance and evil, but there are also truth and goodness, and whereas ignorance and evil tend to be necessary opposites to better impulses, the real stuff in which reality is rooted is the divine combination of goodness and truth which is God. And so, for the time being, we will stop our somewhat rambling musings on the disturbing presence of evil in this world and return to the healing presence of Jesus.

When Zebedee first met Jesus, he thought of Him not as a healer, but as a stealer. Jesus stole his most valuable possessions, his two sons. That day on the beach when they had been working on their nets, James and John had left him and gone off with Jesus. Zebedee experienced despair, but a few years later, after Jesus had risen and been proclaimed, Zebedee's heart filled with pride, as he realized that God had called his sons to be among His first Christian priests. Jesus never came by to apologize to Zebedee for depriving him of his boys and Zebedee understood why He did not. It was because these boys were never actually his. They were always God's, and when God called them away, it was because he, Zebedee, had fulfilled his parental trust. So, a little late, but still with pride, he said, "Take them, Lord. You too can be proud of them." And God surely was, and of their father, too.

As was pointed out earlier, Jesus put great emphasis upon God's love for mankind and upon our consequent responsibility to do our best to come to know and love God. When first enunciated by Jesus, this was a radical concept, as was His statement that we ought to address God as "Father." Now we can look back and reflect upon that revelation by God that He is a loving father. God said to a handful of representative men, "I love you and I want your love." But how do you love a spirit? Well, with great difficulty. That is why God invites you and me to know and love Him in and through Jesus. I hope that by this time you have come to love the Jesus of these pages, at least in the same way as you might come to love a character in an historical play or novel. I'm sure that Jesus would want to be loved in this way, but not only in this way. God cannot be relegated to history. God is. So too, Jesus is. We cannot go to Capernaum and see Him in the synagogue, because He was crucified, died and was buried and is now with the Father in that so-called glorified state, the nature of which is beyond our experience or comprehension. Jesus has moved outside of time and space as we know it, but we still have several direct connections to Him. One of these is through each other. Jesus identified with each one of us in a truly intimate way when He told us that whatever service we performed for the least glamorous among us, we were, in fact, doing to and for Him. This is God identifying with His creatures whom He made in His own image. This is God saying to us, "You want to love me? Then love Jesus, but love and render service to your brothers and sisters in Christ as well." Jesus said, "Love each other as I love each one of you. Let the love that you have for each other be the principal sign of your love for me." The bottom line is this: Jesus, who is God, wishes to give tangible expression of His love for me primarily through YOU. You can refuse to cooperate and, in so doing, paralyse God's loving hand. You can refuse to cooperate, but in so doing, you are making a clear statement that, regardless of what label you would like to wear, you do not love God. That is the extent to which God has identified Himself with humankind, with every blessed one of us. Needless to say, as our awareness and understanding of this disturbing reality increases, so does our responsibility.

A story is told of a seminary in the United States which was heavily damaged by fire. The great damage was to the Chapel. Retrieved from the ruins of the Sanctuary was the large wooden Crucifix which had hung over the main Altar. The knees and the elbows of the Corpus were charred, but the head and centre section remained untouched by the flames. When the Chapel was reconstructed, they took the Corpus, with its blackened, stunted limbs, fastened it to a new Cross and hung it over the new Altar. Beneath it they installed a plaque which read as follows, "You are My hands and My feet."

The apostle, Paul, described his response to life with these words, "Here I am, Lord, at your disposal, for I am whatever I am, by the grace of God." For Paul to have said that, he had to believe that God was involved with him . . . not just with mankind in general, but with him. We must believe that too, or else we run the risk of reading this book as observers, rather than as participants. The God in whose image we are made, the God whose will keeps us in existence, the God who made Himself known and understood in and through Jesus, has made it clear that our main purpose on earth is to guide each other toward truth and to sustain each other through loving, sharing concern. Whether you are pauper or king, that is your principle role as a human being. So often when we are led to reflect upon this fundamental bond, we become uncomfortable and hide behind our lack of influence, our social impotence, our "unfortunate" need to concentrate on other things and a hundred and one other reasons why the work of Jesus, the spreading of the kingdom, is best left to others, who are "far more suited," or "far more worthy." "I am whatever I am, by the grace of God." Believe that and forget the rest. Then, from sickbed, office, kitchen, pulpit, police car, flight deck, classroom, playground, park bench or courthouse, take the opportunities as they present themselves. Make the effort to encourage and support, to forgive and heal, to understand other people's motives, fears and frustrations, and to respond to hostility with calmness and reason. Make the effort to notice other people, to welcome them, compliment them. Leave judgement to God. For any of us to be critics, especially self-appointed critics, is to walk a very dangerous path. Love heals and builds. It doesn't bruise and break down. What we are talking about here is not an accumulation of points based upon a series of good deeds leading toward some qualification. Rather, what is expected is that we develop an attitude toward God and each other that is in harmony with reality.

Unfortunately, human nature as we know it, is a crippled version of what God wanted it to be. We have but to look around us and see the disordered way in which we tend to function in relation to each other and our environment to recognize that all is not well. The Book of Genesis helps us to understand what happened and why it is that we are not by nature good and whole. Genesis tells us that from the dawn of history, humanity abused its liberty, setting itself against God in an effort to find fulfilment apart from God. We are told how God, having created man and woman, saw that they were good. But then the man, Adam, rejected God and tried to become His equal. This rejection we call "Original Sin." As a result of his sin, Adam felt alienated from God and tried to hide from Him. Adam blamed the woman, Eve, and Eve blamed the being, in the form of a serpent, who tempted her. The distortion of relationships had begun. Those who followed in Adam's line inherited his fallen nature. In the very next generation, Cain murdered his brother, Abel. Chaos again came to creation as man tried once again to gain an equal footing with God. He built a tower reaching toward Heaven and different groups competed with each other for prime places in the tower. All communication broke down, as, in rejecting God, man moved on to reject his fellow man. And so a world of beauty was deformed by sin with the active participation of him whom Jesus called "the Prince of Darkness": the angel who defied God long before Adam walked the earth, Satan. The historical reality of original sin has coloured human existence from Adam onward. As Father Richard P. McBrien explains in his scholarly and highly-recommended two-volume work entitled "Catholicism," we inherit a damaged human nature, not because of who we are, but because of what we are. We are not isolated units, but members of the one human race sharing in the one human nature which was passed on in a damaged state by our first parents. It is from the effects of this state that Jesus Christ has redeemed us and as we will see more clearly later, the same oneness of humanity which causes us to suffer the effects of Adam's defeat also enables us to receive the fruits of Christ's victory. There is but one human nature in which we all share and that nature has been radically affected by both Adam and Jesus, who, for this reason, is often referred to as the "new Adam."

Paul said, "I am what I am, by the grace of God." What would I be without God's grace, or, in other words, without His self-communication? Simply a son of Adam, forever hopelessly crippled by a damaged nature. And so, what is it that I am, in fact, by this grace of God? I am still crippled by a damaged nature, but no longer hopelessly so, because although one with Adam in nature and sin, I am now one with Christ, who has incorporated me into His act of love, which has the capacity to swallow all, and every sin. In other words, I am redeemed. And so, Paul was able to tell the Romans that from day to day we freely ratify our state of original sin by means of personal sin, or we freely ratify our redeemed condition by faith, hope and charity.

We will soon return to the subject of our redemption, but for now, let us refocus our attention on the days before Calvary, as we complete our re-examination of Jesus in the light of His Divinity.

Chapter XIII

Jesus broke a lot of rules and ignored many longstanding traditions. He did not do so in order to bait the Pharisees, nor to attract to His entourage a particular type of person. Jesus had great respect for the Law of Moses, as well as for legal codes, such as those governing soldiers and even slaves. But He did insist that for laws to be valid, they must exist to serve people, not just burden them. The Sabbath, He said, was made for man, not vice versa. He also made it clear that all laws took a back seat to the law of charity, and that when charity demanded it, we should not hesitate to break established law, no matter what the cost. Remember when He spoke with, consoled and touched the leper? Remember when He let His disciples pick corn on the Sabbath and allowed them to eat without first going through the prescribed ritual washing? Remember when He cured the sick on the Sabbath? In each case, this was God teaching us a lesson on the subject of law. He was also saying a good deal about how He judges us. The main criterion is clearly charity: do we love as He loves? How different this is from the way we judge each other. I admit it would be hard for civil and criminal courts to base all their judgements on the law of charity. They, after all, cannot read the hearts of men and women as God does. But the fact remains that there is no such thing as true justice without charity.

It has always been a great source of consolation to me and, I believe, to many whose confessions I have heard, to be reminded that God judges us not by how well we do, but by how hard we try. To do otherwise would be nothing less than a mockery of charity. Yet, how do we habitually judge each other? Did you win? Did you sell it? Were you successful? Did you finish on time? Did you convince them? We have so much to learn, but we have the best of teachers: God, in the person of Jesus. After His Resurrection, what was the first thing Jesus said to Peter? Was it, "Peter, you are hopeless. Even when I warned you, you still wound up denying me three times. You are just a lot of talk?" No. What He said was, "Peace be with you," and then He gave Peter the power to forgive other people in Jesus' name. Jesus knew Peter always gave his best.

I laugh as I think back to Zaccheus perched in the tree. Do you remember Jesus' reaction? It tells us so much about God. Zaccheus was a senior tax collector. If Jesus had ridiculed him, it would have delighted the crowds. But He did not. He behaved as if Zaccheus had every reason to be up in the tree and He rewarded his good will by asking to share his home for the night. Stop for a moment and picture this scene one more time. See Jesus with His arm around Zaccheus' shoulder, slowly walking up the private roadway that led to his fashionable home. Zaccheus, tickled pink, his fondest dream more than realized: Jesus and His apostles were to be his guests for the night! Could there be a greater honour? If asked that question, Zaccheus might well have replied, "a greater honour? The only greater honour would be to have Yahweh Himself dwell in my house, making it the Holy of Holies." Little did he know . . .

I am sure that as the years passed, Zaccheus became a devoted follower of the risen Lord, that he, unlike so many of us, never again thought of God as remote and distant from the affairs of ordinary people. Until the moment of his death, Zaccheus treasured the words spoken by his Saviour as he entered his home. "This day salvation has come to this house, for the Son of Man has come to seek and save that which was lost." At that time, outside, the crowd grumbled amongst themselves, asking, did Jesus know who and what Zaccheus was? Why would He associate with such a disreputable shark? Why indeed?

He had entered Jerusalem for the last time. The welcome from the populace had been warm and exuberant. It was Passover time and Jesus and His eleven remaining apostles were gathered about a large table in a rented room. Before them lay everything necessary for the traditional Passover supper. Jesus, we are told, had looked forward to this night for a long time. He knew that He was going to face torture and death within a few hours, but still, He was content. This was not because He had confidence that His divine powers would make the torturers' work ineffective, allowing Him to fake His agony for the sake of history. Far from it. He was content because the gift of His life was going to be very costly, very real, very meaningful. In short, He was going to suffer. His human nature would see to that and His divine nature would respect it. But His suffering would be like no other, because it would show just how far He, God, was prepared to go to prove His love for mankind. Jesus was content for another reason, too. He was content because He had decided upon a way in which He could relate intimately, for all time to come, to any human being who desired such intimacy.

No priest, prophet or king who came before Him could have done what He was about to do. He was making it possible for us to enter into a flesh-and-blood relationship with Him, with God. He knew that, generally speaking, no bond on earth was closer than that of family, whether it be through adoption or by virtue of flesh and blood. He did not want anyone to be more closely related, more intimately united to those eleven men, and their wives and children, than He was. But beyond that, far beyond that, He was, even at that moment, feeling the same attachment to you and to me, and He wanted to establish and maintain no less close a relationship with us. How could He do this? Taking the bread into His hands, He blessed it and distributed it saying, "Take and eat. This is my body which will be given up for you." Years before, He had said, "The bread that I will give you will be my flesh for the life of the world." Now in the upper room, God was fulfilling His promise. Shortly after, He did the same with a cup of wine, proclaiming it to be the chalice of His blood. To eat that bread and to drink that wine was to enter into a flesh-and-blood relationship with Jesus Christ . . . with God Himself. The apostles knew that they were making sacred history, but how sacred they could not even guess. Only after Pentecost would they fully realize what had happened during that Passover supper. What Jesus did could only have been done by God, the author of all relationships.

Throughout the history of Israel, covenants or agreements were signed in blood, the symbol of life. Jesus explained to His apostles that a new Covenant was about to be signed, and once more, in blood; a Covenant between God and His people, signed not with the blood of goats or lambs, but with the blood of a man. And at the same time, although the apostles could not grasp it, signed with the blood of God Himself. The terms of this new Covenant between God and man would involve forgiveness of those who turned their backs on God, provided that forgiveness was humbly sought. To those who would respect divine authority and attempt to live according to the teachings of Jesus, God would grant a continuing unity with Him, which would begin in this life, but remain intact through death and extend into a new and everlasting life.

Of all of earth's creatures, only man is designed to pass through this world into the next. Only man is designed for eternity. To live as if it all began and ended here makes as much sense as using a 747 as a highway cruiser.

The next day, the sentence of Rome and of the people of Jerusalem was carried out. Jesus was executed. And so the wood of the crib became the wood of the Cross. The joyful young mother became our Lady of Sorrows. The infant of yesterday cried out, "My God, my God, why have you forsaken me?" No one doubted that they were seeing a man suffer both physical and mental agony. So great was His suffering that He felt as though His own divine nature had betrayed Him. In keeping with the nature of perfect love, He emptied Himself completely. After all of the hopes, all of the promises, it was over. He who encouraged and healed so many was nailed to a cross. Murdered by public demand. God's perfect idea of Himself, having been made man, was murdered. The flesh and blood which He longed to unite in fraternal relationship to each of us was torn and spilled. Surely the time had come for God to turn away from man, but that did not happen. God's love for man could never be so shallow. The necessary ingredient of love which we call respect demanded, as it were, that God never do anything to lessen the foundation of human dignity . . . free will. For various reasons, some powerful and not so powerful people decreed that Jesus must die. Others, a little less influential, clearly willed otherwise. The former prevailed. But for the latter, there was yet to come the dawn. The dawn of Easter.

We of this century have seen the dawn of Easter. So why don't we wipe forever from our collective memories the gross indecency of Calvary and leap from the hopeful joy of Christmas to the triumph of Easter? Because that is not the way it is. We cannot do this, because the reality is that without the Friday of death, there can be no Sunday of life, not only for Jesus, but for us as well. The very nature of the real world demands that we confront evil. The priceless message of Good Friday is that because of Christ's ultimate triumph, we can be sure that if we are united to Him in word and action, we will emerge victorious, triumphant, free, whole, one with goodness and truth. No matter how deep the pits we fall, or are pushed, into, no matter how long or how dark the tunnels, in and through Him, we shall overcome. He went willingly to the cross because He knew that in the course of life you and I would face evil, pain, despair and finally death. He knew that you and I would face the spectre of terminal illness, old age, loneliness, terrorism, natural disasters, the suffering of children and brutality in all of its forms, for these are all part of life. They are mysteriously wrapped up in the essence of power, in the temporal evolution of creation, in the nature of free will and, especially, in the effects of original sin. That evil exists, we have no doubt. As to why it exists, we can, as we have seen, only speculate. But we do know that because of Jesus' personal encounter and ultimate victory, no manifestation of evil can be said to be final. That is why the

Friday of infamy is known as Good Friday.

And now, as promised, we will spend some time looking at the whole concept of redemption, which seems to pit a poor innocent Jesus against an unyielding, demanding Father, with us somewhere in the middle and somehow the cause of it all.

The redemptive sacrifice of Jesus has been given a lot of attention in recent years by some very scholarly people. Their efforts have helped me toward what I believe to be a better understanding of Good Friday.

The first Christians were convinced that Jesus would return to mark the end of time within a few years of His Resurrection. Because of this expectation, they were not very inclined to meditate upon and consequently develop a theology of the Crucifixion. Their focus was from the Resurrection to the second coming of Christ and all that they believed that to imply. Only later, when they began with the help of the Holy Spirit to perceive that the end of time was by no means imminent did they begin to seek a deeper understanding of the significance of Jesus' passion and death.

Jesus said that He would give His life as a ransom for many. I believe that we know more precisely what that means today than we did even thirty or forty years ago. I am theologically conservative and tend to be suspicious of theories which disturb traditional thought patterns, but, at the same time, I deeply appreciate fresh scholarly insight, especially when it tends to eliminate, or, at least, lessen, apparent contradictions in our understanding of God's ways. The way that I have come to appreciate Jesus' redemptive sacrifice is as follows.

Jesus could not have avoided the gradual alienation of the authorities and at the same time remained authentic in His words and deeds. From day one it should have been clear that, sooner or later, He would be removed from the scene. His challenge to the status quo was simply too powerful and too direct to be ignored by those with vested interests. The fact that He went all the way to dying on the cross is clear proof that He believed deeply in what He had said and done and, above all, that He was totally dedicated to those who heard and heeded His voice. As John remarked, "To give one's life is the strongest possible witness of one's love." And Jesus did give His life. He could at any time have called the whole thing off and saved Himself. But He did not and this was obviously not for His own sake. So He gave His life as a lasting and convincing statement of His sincerity and His love for His fellow man. But He knew when He began and He knew on the cross that there was a force at work which, although not as powerful as the ultimate force, Divine Love, was nevertheless a force to be reckoned with, as the only power capable of defeating it was that same Divine Love.

The force of which we speak is sin. That force is at work in each one of us, demanding that we care for ourselves at the expense of God and others. Its antithesis is caring for God and others at the expense of self: in other words, charity. Sin, then, is the flip-side of love. There is nothing very mysterious about sin. It is the manifestation of our fallen nature and our abuse of free will. It is a failure to live up to the terms of the Covenant between God and man which was instituted by Jesus at the Last Supper and sealed, on Jesus' part, by His death and resurrection, and on our part, by our personal dedication to God and gospel values and observances. When we break the Covenant, it is only logical that, providing we are penitent, we seek God's forgiveness, for God, after all, is the other party in the agreement. When we are forgiven, we are redeemed, we are saved. From what? From the effects of our wounded nature and from ourselves, from our shortsightedness, which so often makes us slaves to our appetites and illusions.

Slaves were traditionally freed when someone ransomed them. So, we metaphorically speak of Jesus in His supreme act of love as having ransomed us: metaphorically, because this was definitely not a price somehow demanded of Jesus by the

Father. Redemption and ransom are metaphorical terms in this context, just as are slavery and bondage. It is simply a way of saying that Jesus' death and resurrection constitute irrefutable evidence of God's endless, loving patience with all of us. He will never refuse to forgive and therefore, as long as we can muster the sincerity and the humility to say, "I am sorry," sin will never get the best of us. With God's help, our better side will always land face-up. That is salvation. That is redemption.

We have spoken of the powerful message contained in the way Jesus died. It should be said that the basic reason for His dying at all was so that He could rise again, as He had promised, and enter into new life, thus proving that His promise of life after death for Himself and, by association, for us all, was not just empty words. In order for us to have hope, there had to be what Paul called, "a firstborn from the dead." That was Jesus. Our hope is made all the more realistic and attainable because we are assured that the gates of heaven are wide enough to accommodate all of us, no matter how much evil we have done, how hateful we have become. His love is still greater and He will, if given the slightest chance, forgive, redeem and ransom you and me.

From the time we are introduced to Jesus, our loving Saviour, He says to us repeatedly, "Stick with me and I will help you." He helps us by communicating with us on the spiritual level, by what we might call putting ideas into our heads and by giving us peace of mind when we need it most. His voice is so gentle that we rarely recognize it, and there is no doubt in my mind that He inspires others to help us with a word of advice, a shared tear or a joyful hug. All of this is day-by-day redemption. It is a powerful process. The most powerful process on earth and it alone keeps the world from going completely berserk and devouring itself.

* * *

133

Sometimes when we read the Gospels, we tend to forget that they were written for second-generation Christians. These Christians lacked the direct, tangible experience of Jesus, which was the unique privilege of the first Christians. This second generation of Christians was dependent upon the credibility of those who personally experienced the risen Christ. For many, the witness of the generation before them was the sole basis of their faith. The problem was that were they to discover that one of the apostles was a drunk or a child molester, the whole fabric of their Christian faith would crumble. Modern day parallels attesting to the vulnerability of the foundations of faith are legion. How many people have turned away from God because they have been scandalized by the frailty of His servants? What the New Testament authors were trying to do for second generation Christians, as well as for the rest of us, was to plug us into the ongoing reality of the Christ event, so that the witness of others, while potentially positive and important, would not be the only reason why we today declare Jesus Christ to be the son of God and risen from the dead. The event of which we speak, the Christ event, is, in summary, the incarnation of the second person of the Blessed Trinity, who chose to incorporate us into His life, death and Resurrection, thereby establishing a new and significant relationship between man and God. Thus, if we want to, we can have Jesus as our companion through life into death and through His power, beyond death into eternity. I am talking about not just the memory of Jesus, but Jesus here and now. As He said to His disciples, "I will be with you for all time, right up to the end of the world." Jesus is present, not as He was between His Resurrection and Ascension, for that was a special manifestation for special people during a special time in history. He is now present in the Holy Spirit, for where the Spirit is, there too are Jesus and the Father.

Do not think of the Blessed Trinity as some kind of royal family, with each member off on his or her daily appearances and assignments. There is only one God, Father, Son and Holy Spirit. Some mistakenly see in the Trinity something akin to a law firm. The Father handles creation and all cases connected with it, such as environment and rainfall. The Son, having had hands-on experience with humans, is the tough attorney who cannot be fooled, while the Holy Spirit is soft-hearted and gives us the occasional hint as to which way to move.

When we speak of efficient causality, we mean that there exists in God only one power, one will, one presence and one activity. Yet, the Second Vatican Council taught that as a community, we are called by the Father to carry forward the work of the Son with the sanctifying power of the Holy Spirit. Now this does not imply three distinct areas of responsibility, but rather, three distinct ways of God's being present to us; three different ways of God subsisting in the godhead itself; three in God, to whom we can say "YOU." Father McBrien sums it up in these words: "What the mystery and doctrine of the Trinity mean, when all is said and done, is that the God who created us, who sustains us, who will judge us, and who will give us eternal life is not a God infinitely removed from us. On the contrary, our God is a god of absolute proximity; a god who is communicated truly in the flesh, in history, within our human family, and a god who is present in the spiritual depths of our existence, as well as in the core of our unfolding human history; as the source of enlightenment and community."

Do you remember Thomas? The world still thinks of him as "Doubting Thomas," because he had to have his own experience of the risen Lord before he was prepared to say his personal "Amen." Do you recall the scene when Jesus invited Thomas to touch Him and believe? To his subsequent profession of faith, Jesus responded with a word of praise for those who would come along later and believe in Him, although they would not be able to touch Him. Theirs, ours, would be the privilege of being touched by Him. Few of us are sufficiently sensitive to His touch, so we need to heighten our consciousness of God's presence. We should not force God to compete for our time and attention. We must stop talking long enough to listen, stop anticipating the future for long enough to live the present. We will find special moments when God is very real to us. We are no less significant to the risen Christ than was Thomas in his day. What Jesus did for Thomas, He wants to do for us. Our faith is not supposed to rest upon what was, but rather, on what continues to be. Christ is risen. What this means, of course, is that we must abandon all notions of God as being a distant majesty, observing us from on high. Rather, God is father, helper and liberator. He is mercifully present to all of us. His kingdom, although not fully established, is now on earth, and we can be part of its evolution.

Chapter XIV

It is not my intention to go into the vast subject of the Church, its historic beginnings at Pentecost, its sacramental system and its relevance to modern man. To do so would be to go well beyond the original intent and purpose of this book. Perhaps we will soon be able to explore these and other topics together under another cover. The time has come, then, to tie together a few loose ends.

.....

We have already observed the effects of Pentecost on Peter and the others, as, permeated and illuminated by the Spirit which is God, they joyfully proclaimed the risen Lord. It was on that note, in fact, that we began our consideration of the Christ event. From that vantage point, we looked back in time to John the Baptizer and his early ministry, and went on to meet Jesus and accompany Him, with the intention of getting to know Him. After His Resurrection, convinced of His identity as Messiah and divinity, we looked back once again, to briefly consider what we had, perhaps unwittingly, learned about God as we had come to know Jesus. As getting to know God is the expressed purpose of this work, I will conclude by trying to shed some light on a few particular areas which I believe to be vital to our appreciation of the God of goodness and truth.

....

God made the following promise: "To those who listen to my voice and follow my direction, I will grant eternal life." What is this "eternal life?" Is it an endless form of what we now experience? "No," says John. "This is eternal life: that they know the one true God and Jesus, whom He has sent." Since we already know something of the Father and Jesus, it appears that eternal life begins here, in coexistence with temporal life. And so, heaven can begin on earth if we hear and heed the word of God. We can conclude, then, that heaven is not primarily a place, but, rather, a condition: a condition or state of intimacy with God in and through Christ. Now this, in turn, suggests a state of unity, binding together all those who share the common condition of unity with Christ. If I am united to Christ and you are united to Christ, then we have a common bond. We are, as Paul reminds us, "brothers and sisters in Christ." This relationship between each of us and God is obviously based upon a spiritual, not a biological, foundation and what this means is that it, therefore, cannot be terminated by death. As the funeral liturgy tells us, in death, life is changed, not ended. Life is changed in that we are no longer a flesh-and-blood-entity. We do not eat. We do not sleep. We do not go to work, raise children or go south in the winter. But none of this affects the relationship which we are discussing. This is what Jesus was demonstrating to us through His Resurrection. His life was changed, but not ended, and His relationship to us, in all its truly significant aspects, remains unchanged. In other words, if Jesus were two thousand years old and living in your house, His relationship with you would be no more significant than it is now. The life that we begin in Baptism, and the relationship that we forge with God and with others united to Him, is simply not subject to death. Therefore, after we die, we can expect some kind of relationship with many of the people whom we knew and loved on earth, especially those with whom we shared the common bond of love for, and fidelity toward, Jesus Christ. It is in knowing and loving that we are said to be God's image. So it only makes sense that heaven consists of knowing and loving God and each other to the fullest. In heaven, truth and goodness will be the very essence of our lives, as has always been the case with God.

Being creatures endowed with free will, we are, of course, capable of alienating ourselves from God, of literally damning ourselves by what we choose or neglect to do. In the process, we also risk alienating ourselves from those who have opted for intimacy with God. This is Hell. The split begins in this life and becomes permanent in the next. If heaven begins on earth, so, too, does hell. Now, to qualify for hell, the alienation must be complete. Because of Christ's loving sacrifice, anything less than total alienation will ensure our ultimate salvation. In other words, you do not have to be all that good to get to heaven. That is why He created us. "Thou hast made us for Thyself," said Augustine, "and our hearts are restless until they rest in Thee." It is too bad that most of us are not a little keener to get to heaven. We know what makes us happy here on earth and we are not so sure that the purely spiritual versions of those joys will compare favourably. As a recent article in Newsweek magazine put it, "The hell of thinking about heaven is that we cannot imagine or trust a love that surpasses our own understanding," to which I say, "Amen."

....

One often hears the term "blind faith" as being characteristic of believing Christians. It is a term which I resent, in that it implies irrational faith. What we believe might well be beyond reason, but never contrary to it.

Reality, as I see it, is that the spirit of God within us, the spirit of goodness and truth, urges us to seek truth and helps us to recognize it, blessing us with an inexplicable sense of certainty. This is not BLIND faith, but rather, INSPIRED faith. It is the result of having God within us or God present to us. It may be very mysterious; however, so is electricity, but that does not stop us from seeing the light. When I think of faith, I often think of Christmas, the birthday of Jesus, God-become-man for the love of us. God, the ultimate reality, the prime mover, the Creator of the universe, the omnipotent, the eternal, somehow condensed Himself into the body and soul of an infant boy. Hard to imagine? It is impossible to imagine! And that is why believing it can be a problem.

As we observed much earlier, humanity cannot contain its infinite Creator in its finite mind. Therefore, there is a danger that it will reject Him altogether. The finite says to the infinite, "I cannot define you. Therefore, you do not exist." The material says to the spiritual, "I cannot smell, hear, taste, see or feel you. Therefore, you do not exist." And yet, some of us can and do proclaim, "I believe in God. I believe in the divinity of Jesus Christ," demonstrating that we are capable of responding to a source of conviction that is more fundamental, more basic, than reason or even the senses. In fact, we are responding to that spirit within us which, as St. Paul tells us, cries out in recognition, "Father." And so, if someone were to ask you why it is that you believe in God, the Father almighty, Creator of heaven and earth, and in Jesus Christ, His only Son, our Lord, would you be at a loss for a convincing reply? Of course you would. Because the truth is, we believe and yet we do not fully understand. But do not let that bother you, because everyone has his or her concept of what constitutes ultimate reality, and few have as much understanding of the whys and wherefores of their god as we have of ours.

It would seem that the bottom line for everyone is faith. But faith in what? Our creed proclaims the one God of the Judeo-Christian tradition. The other gods are proclaimed in other creeds, enunciated in sanctuaries which range from homes to schools, to banks, to hospitals, to taverns. Some of these gods are said, like ours, to transcend the material world, but most do not even pretend to do so. All of these gods are difficult to define, not because they are infinite, but rather because they are finite and dependent upon the latest political, ethical, social and economic theories. And so, their adherents, when asked to explain their god, have much the same problem as we do, for they too, believe without fully understanding. They, too, have faith, but faith in what? All of this brings us back to Christmas, which is, for some, an annual commercial bonanza, for others, a time for a family reunion, and for yet others, a happy day or a sad and lonely day. But when all is said and done, Christmas has but one true meaning. It is our God's only son's birthday. Now, some of the other gods have appropriated it as one of their days too, so do not let their voices confuse you, leaving you to wonder whether your God and Christmas are not just part of a great fable, the credibility of which is slowly crumbling before the onslaught of human genius and productivity, which are two of the newer and perhaps, more with-it gods. Our God has always been hard to believe in. Like Jesus' young mother, we do not fully comprehend and yet, we believe. This is faith, but not just any faith. This is divine faith. It is the result of our hearing God speaking to Himself within us.

....

We have spoken of God as creator and sustainer, so we accept the fact that we are dependent upon His will in order to remain in existence. You may want to review our decision about that if the idea has become a little hazy. The question that we are all led to ask, sooner or later, is to what extent does God control my destiny? We must begin with the fact that nothing is hidden from God, whether it be in our past, present or future. To God, all things are "now," for He is not subject to time or motion. As Jesus said, "Before Abraham came to be, I am." God then, sees my entire life span in, as it were, one glance. He knows, for example, where, when and how I will die. Does this in some way affect my freedom? Is my freedom limited to the freedom to follow a preordained path, like a train on a track laid out by someone else? I think not. It does not necessarily follow that since God knows what is going to happen, He must be causing it, or in other words, willing it to happen. I think we can agree that each of us has but one future, be it good or bad, short or long. That future is going to happen simply because it is my future. God sees it, but it is brought about by many factors, such as my decisions, the impact upon my life of other peoples' decisions, illness, accidents, and so on. If God manifests His power directly, it is a miracle and miracles do happen. But it appears that having given us free will, He generally respects our freedom to stumble along. And while He gives us His help in many ways and through countless means, He should not be expected to interfere directly.

Let me give you an example: I remember going to a funeral parlour where the focal point of everyone's attention was the sealed casket of a five-year-old boy. I overheard a well-meaning person say to the distraught mother, "Take courage. It is God's will." I then took the parents to one side and said to them, "If God willed that your child be hit by a car last Monday, then I, here and now, reject that God. What kind of cruel, monster god could will such a tragedy? The reality was that a man had an argument with a customer, went to a bar and got drunk, got into his car and ran down a little boy. The poor man certainly did not want to kill the child. He probably did not even want to get drunk. It was a tragic accident for which he, nevertheless, had to accept responsibility. Where was God in all of this? He was respecting everyone's freedom and He was there at that fatal moment to receive the little victim into eternal happiness. And I believe He was with me as I tried to bring His comfort to the bereaved family and later, to the driver of the car.

God is not a master puppeteer, manipulating us all on the end of a string. Contrary to the opinion of some very pious people, God is not in control of what is going on. This is because He loves us and the freedom that love gives is for the "other" to be in control. The dignity with which He has invested us demands freedom, responsibility and interdependence. This means that we are vulnerable to all kinds of malice, stupidity and carelessness. As I see it, the opposite scenario would be truly bizarre. That is, a god who consistently rescued all children up to a certain age from fatal accidents. The last thing I want to do is make light of this type of happening. The desolation and hurt that a parent must feel boggles the mind and breaks the heart, and I have no doubt that the urge to lash out in anger and frustration is overpowering. I think that in such circumstances it makes more sense to blame God, to, as it were, damn God, than to calmly attribute the whole thing to His mysterious, yet benevolent, will. The former reaction can be dealt with more easily. Sometimes all it takes is a hug. It has been my experience that the latter interpretation is tenaciously held onto because for many people, God is totally mysterious, unknowable and aloof. This is tragic, and I have written this book with these people in mind.

There might, however, have been another set of circumstances in which it could have been said that God saved the child from being run over. But this would require one of several possible changes in the scenario. For example, someone could have responded to the urging of the Holy Spirit, whether recognized as such or not, and made certain that the intoxicated man did not drive his car. I believe it to be probable that prior to every tragedy which is caused by human weakness, God does give us a chance to reconsider; however, it is never to the point of lessening our freedom. That chance may come several steps before the event occurs. But I believe that it is always offered somewhere along the line. I cannot help but wonder how many times I may have been the chosen instrument of intervention, but have failed because, for some unacceptable reason, I did not want to involve myself. It is a sobering thought.

....

We have come to know a God who is the essence of goodness and truth. Our faith in this God, although firm in its basic premise, still seeks understanding and clarification through reflection and, hopefully, dialogue with one another. We cannot take our faith for granted. We must dwell and pray upon it. In this way, God communicates Himself to us. The fact that you even picked up this book indicates that you are aware of this. We also need to develop a sense of trust where God is concerned. We know Him to be good and so, when faced with an evil that we cannot understand or rationalize, we must train ourselves to be comfortable with that basic posture of trust. We do not have an answer for every question and we have ample evidence that God's ways are not our ways. So trust becomes the bottom line for the believer in the one true God. But why? Why does God not step in forcefully from time to time and make Himself obvious, even if this entails some small cost to our freedom? I don't know. Trust Him. Why does He not halt the progress of disease in this or that person? We know He is good. Trust Him. Why do so many evil people seem to prosper? We know that He is just. Trust Him. Trust that, as John tells us, the time will come when God Himself will "wipe away every tear from our eyes, and there shall be no more death or mourning, crying out, or pain, for the former world will have passed away."

An important way to develop one's trust in God is through prayer. Now that may sound like putting the cart before the horse, but this is not the case. Earlier, we touched upon the subject of extrasensory perception: how the knowing, loving self which is the core of each of us is clearly capable of communicating at a level independent of the senses. It seems reasonable that this would be the route through which God directly communicates with us, for He is, after all, pure spirit and we, as a consequence of being made in His image, have a complementary spiritual dimension. And so we are encouraged to open and prepare our minds and our wills for His motion toward us. This divine action, followed by our response to it, is the dialogue of prayer. It always begins with God. Whenever we pray, it is in response to God's motion toward us. No matter how it may seem otherwise, we are not the initiators. You might say that God is always speaking to us and it is up to us to tune in. The saint hears His voice and none other.

Have you ever noticed that Churches, no matter how short of funds, never resort to leasing out their inner walls for advertising placards, as is done in city buses and hockey arenas? This is because Churches are already full of signs; sometimes only the signs of silence and space, but often, too, sacred art and architecture. This is so that when we enter the Church, our minds and hearts will be drawn to the reality of God's universal presence and we will be moved to listen to Him. It is called placing ourselves in the presence of God and it can be done anywhere, although it is best done when the potential distractions are at a minimum. As we can expect, there are countless so-called methods of prayer. Apart from praising God and giving thanks for each moment of life, I like to simply think things through in God's presence. By "things" I mean whatever concerns me. The conclusions I reach, the attitudes I develop, the resolutions I formulate are good and true; in other words, of God to the extent that I am truly open. From this it should be evident that it is within the nature of prayer to renew, strengthen and change us, not to inform, convince and change God.

An analogy that recently came to mind has proven to be of considerable value in my personal search for the essence of prayer. I have come to imagine God's constant caring presence as though it were a flame that everyone carries within themselves, sometimes knowingly, sometimes unknowingly.

Since God is everywhere, His supporting presence is, in one way or another, everywhere, but it is localized in an intense, mystical, caring fashion within the souls of men and women. It is God's will that every person on earth be His torch-bearer. That flame within us, first brought from possibility to actuality through the Sacrament of Baptism, is nourished and strengthened by the Eucharist, penance, good works, caring thoughts and by praising and thanking God.

When, as Christians, we are Christ to others, we share the flame. Just as a burning stick is taken from an established fire in order to strengthen another "hearth," so we share the Divine presence in order to strengthen another "heart."

A significant way of being Christ to others is to pray for them as Jesus prayed for His disciples and for us. Our prayer, no matter how spasmodic or how distracted, when offered through Christ, our Lord cannot but intensify the flame and add to its strength and brightness in the souls of those for whom we pray. Among the practical effects are insight, comfort and conversion.

Remember St. Monica's prayers for her son, Augustine. The process may be slow, but it is certain. The key is perseverance. Think of the value your prayers can have for the sick, the frightened, the lonely, the betrayed, the misled . . .

This understanding of prayer helps to put flesh and sinew onto the doctrine of the Mystical Body of Christ. In praying for ourselves and for others, we strengthen and invigorate the members, and when our prayer is one of divine praise, we are recognizing that all vitality comes from the head of the body who is Christ.

Thus the greater glory of God, which is the ultimate purpose of creation, is served by our prayers of praise, thanksgiving and petition. Our prayer is not a means of informing God. Our prayer is the spirit fanning the flame. It is a conduit for divine energy; it has no limits, no boundaries. It penetrates the hardest and softest of hearts. It stimulates the deepest and most shallow of intellects, and gives strength and right direction to the weakest and strongest of wills. It is God within us.

....